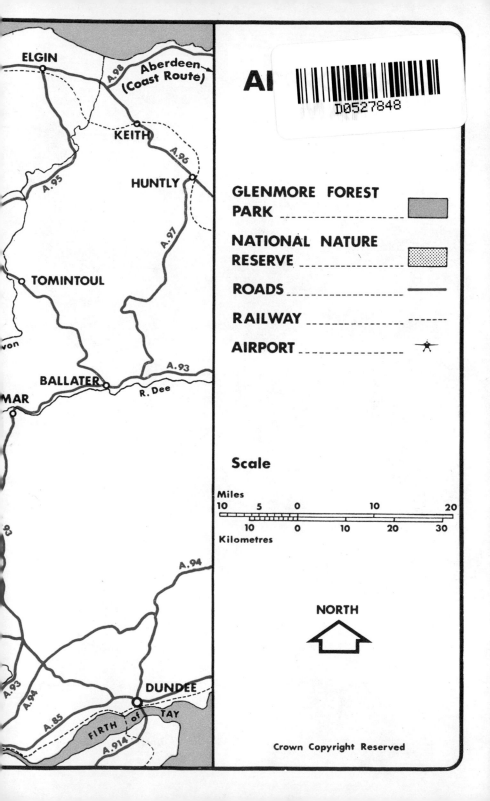

ELGIN

Aberdeen
(Coast Route)

A.98

KEITH

A.96

A.95

HUNTLY

A.97

TOMINTOUL

...von

A.93

BALLATER

R. Dee

...MAR

...93

A.94

A.93

A.94

A.85

DUNDEE

FIRTH of TAY

A.914

A|

D0527848

**GLENMORE FOREST
PARK** _____

**NATIONAL NATURE
RESERVE** _____

ROADS _____ ——

RAILWAY _____ - - - - -

AIRPORT _____ ✈

Scale

Miles
10   5   0   10   20

10   0   10   20   30
Kilometres

NORTH

⬆

GLEN MORE
FOREST PARK
CAIRNGORMS

Looking towards Cairn Lochan from the Pass of Ryvoan

FORESTRY COMMISSION GUIDE

GLEN MORE
FOREST PARK
CAIRNGORMS

Edited by
D. A. WOODBURN, B.Sc
District Officer for Glen More

EDINBURGH
HER MAJESTY'S STATIONERY OFFICE

© *Crown copyright 1975*

First published 1949
Fifth Edition 1975

ISBN 0 11 710128 1

CONTENTS

ACKNOWLEDGMENTS

MR. ROBERT A. INNES, Conservator of Forests for North Scotland, and his staff gave valued assistance throughout the preparation of this Guide. Mr. William Morison, Head Forester at Glen More, contributed a store of local knowledge.

Gordon Harvey of Inverness painted the cover picture.

Colin Gibson, D.A., drew the frontispiece and most of the chapter heading drawings; those for the chapters on History, Old Ways of Life, Plant Life, Forestry and Safety on the Mountains are by Vivien Hislop, D.A.

Professor J. C. Anderson provided the geological map and Mr. P. E. O'Sullivan the diagrams to illustrate the chapter on Loch Morlich. The panorama for the Hill Walks article was prepared by Murray G. Scott and that of the Cairngorm Ski Area by Douglas Godlington.

The topographical maps are based on the Ordnance Survey, by permission of the Controller of Her Majesty's Stationery Office, and were adapted for this Guide by Mrs. Dina MacKay.

The chapter heading verses by William Jeffrey are taken from the poem *Rothiemurchus*, published in *Sea Glimmer* (Maclellan, Glasgow, 1948) and are included by kind permission of Mrs. Jeffrey and the publishers. Thanks are also due to the other poets named, and their publishers, for permission to reproduce their work.

The photographs. Thanks are due to the following photographers who have so ably depicted the Forest Park and its surroundings under the varying moods of season and weather, as well as some of its most charming denizens:

Mr. Robert M. Adam for Plates 1, 2, 16, 17; Mr. W. S. Thomson for Plate 3; Mr. W. A. Poucher for Plates 4, 33, 35, 36, 39; David Hastie for Plate 6; Mr. B. H. Humble for Plates 25, 31, 32, 37, 45, 46.

Her Majesty's Geological Survey for Plates 7, 8; Mr. J. A. McCook for Plates 9, 13, 14, 15, 26, 42, 58, 59, 60, 61, 62, 63; The Forestry Commission for Plate 10; Eric Langmuir for Plates 11, 12, 30, 38, 43, 48, 50; Herbert L. Edlin for Plates 27, 28, 34, 54, 56.

Eric Hosking for Plate 19; J. T. Fisher for Plate 20; Mikel Utsi for Plates 22, 23, 24; Mr. B. Auld for Plate 29; Howard Bell for Plate 40.

Tom Weir for Plate 41; John Cunningham for Plate 44; Inverness-shire Constabulary for Plate 47; Messrs. Valentines of Dundee for Plates 49, 55; Douglas Godlington for Plates 51, 52, 53; Mr. A. L. Hunter for Plate 57.

Peter Thompson for Plate 18; Lea McNally for Plate 21; *The Scotsman* for Plate 5.

FOREWORD
BY ALEXANDER FORSYTH

It is a very great pleasure and honour to be asked to write the fore-word to another revised edition of this well-known, well-used and well-loved guide.

It brings together, in handy form, a variety of concise, useful papers of interest to the public at large, to the holiday tourist and to the specialist. Listed in it are many prime sources of information on the Cairngorms and Glen More, often compiled by experts in their subjects.

With over 50 years of enjoyment in the Highland forests and hills behind me, I am conscious of the changes that have taken place and, indeed, that are always in progress. Natural change is often imperceptible; only detailed records or photographs tell us how much gradual natural change takes place in a relatively short time. Man-made change tends to be more spasmodic and therefore has all the greater an impact. Since change does take place it is important to ponder the cause, the effect, the gain and the loss.

We were still recovering from the sudden changes and losses of war when this guide was first published in 1949, but we looked forward to greater opportunity for all to enjoy better health care, improved education, and more leisure and travel. Part of the latter was the prospect of good company and recreation in the wide open spaces of our land. The replanting of our forests, felled in war time, was well in hand and many development ideas, discussed in the dark years by country lovers, were becoming possible.

By 1966, when the 4th edition was published, we had seen some major development of the imaginative ideas of those who worked to make the Spey Valley come alive again. They saw it as a wonderful area in which to live and which could give opportunity to greater numbers in work and play.

Since then—so unexpectedly to many—the Highlands and Islands have become involved in a brave new world of oil development, with major construction sites on the mainland and in the islands, supply bases and distribution depots. Of course, it has brought people and new job prospects where formerly we had few.

All of these developments have produced pressures on our avail-able outdoor and indoor leisure resources. Much concern has been expressed, particularly about the Cairngorm and Glen More area.

Let me be frank. For the access, enjoyment, and greater fulfilment of the many we have sacrificed some of the peace, quiet and solitude of the few. But we have the living valley, with young people able to come and join our own youth to learn the forests and the hills; to help to mould the old disciplines which we must codify, teach and, perhaps, develop further to care for our environment under today's pressures.

It is clear that, at all levels of public and private life near the great hills and open spaces, there is an appreciation of the fragility of the environment. In parallel with the rush of development there has been a rush—one might almost say rash—of protective thinking from many quarters. Some of it has come from those farthest away from the problems of living and working in the Highlands. Nevertheless, I think we now have not only an understanding and appreciation of the problems, we have the beginnings of major steps forward.

There is a willingness to make greater areas of countryside available to the public. We also have improving transport services and greater mobility—although both can be threatened from time to time by energy crises! We are willing to develop appropriate standards of accommodation, other facilities, access and care. We have a considerable number of publicly supported agencies working closely with local authorities and with private and voluntary organisations to ensure that appropriate discussion takes place, that the right kind of money is available and that the right balance is struck between "keep out" and "come in".

During the programmes of post-war replanting the Forestry Commission also played a major role in developing public interest in, and concern for, our natural resources.

Great experience has been gained in helping the public by provision of information centres, nature trails, caravan and camping sites, and in pioneering new ways of making it possible to cope with more visitors, leading all concerned towards a balanced, enjoyable use of our forest heritage.

In recent months the Commission have produced welcome new plans for additional public access and use of maturing forests and have proposed forest lodges, chalet villages and related facilities—developed in part, I am sure, from Glen More experience.

Glen More has played a great part in Highland history, in forestry, in leisure and also in our scientific pioneering for knowledge, helping to establish at least some of the criteria for the continuing study of many subjects. In its maturity, may we treat it kindly for the enjoyment of forester and scientist, local visitor and holidaymaker, young and old.

Rothiemurchus Forest and the Lairig Ghru

Let the eye at this living instant survey from a vantage point
The swelling majesty of our mountains and their infolded peace,
And take in the rich greenery and warm heath of the forest,
And note how, holding time in suspense,
They absorb all sound into silence, all movement into the trance of stone.

— William Jeffrey

INTRODUCTION

By Professor John Walton

THE establishment of a Forest Park in 1948 by the Forestry
Commission at the Queen's Forest of Glen More extended the parts
of Scotland to which the public has access and in which the country
lover, climber and naturalist can wander in complete freedom.
This freedom, however, carries with it a responsibility to preserve
the beauty and natural treasures of the area, and to guard against
doing anything which will spoil it for others. The Cairngorms, and
particularly the Glen More part of them, are representative of
what is most impressive in the Eastern Highlands. The great precipices and corries round the edge of the summit plateaux, flanked by
the massive slopes of the mountainside, seem to form a gigantic

1

fortress standing firm against the onslaught of the elements. The great granite masses seem rooted and unshakable.

In contrast to this grim splendour of the mountains we have all the beauty of the living world, the alpine and arctic types of flowers, the pinewoods, and, in the centre, that clear and sparkling sheet of water, Loch Morlich.

FEATURES OF INTEREST NEAR THE PARK

LOCH AN EILEIN, 6 miles from Glen More Lodge by a public road B970 running due south from Coylumbridge, deserves a visit for its romantic setting amidst ancient pinewoods that have happily escaped the ravages of the wars. The ruined castle on its islet was founded about the fifteenth century, and extended four times thereafter. It was held by the Mackintoshes before 1539, by the Gordons until 1567, and has since remained in the possession of the Grants.

The Nature Conservancy Council has, with the consent of the owner, Colonel Grant, laid out a nature trail around the loch and renovated an old cottage into an exhibition and display centre This centre is open and staffed during the summer months.

The hill of CRAIGELLACHIE (1,700 feet), commemorated by the Grants' war cry of "Stand fast, Craigellachie!" is well worth ascending for the fine views it commands both up and down Strath Spey, and across to the Cairngorms.

Also within reach of the Park are some of the most remote and beautiful of the Highland straths and glens, particularly those of the Findhorn (Strath Dearn), the Dulnain, the Feshie, and the Tromie. Loch Alvie, Loch Insch, Loch Garten and Loch Pityoulish all lie within a few miles of the Park, and their beautiful tree-clad shores well merit a visit. At Loch Garten ospreys return each year to nest and rear their young in an old pine tree. Visitors are permitted to view them from observation hides erected and wardened by the Royal Society for the Protection of Birds.

The Glen More Forest Park is complementary to the Argyll and the Queen Elizabeth Forest Parks, for the latter are typical of the Western Highlands region, where the mountains are more irregular in form and where the ash and oak woods in the straths take the place of the pine woods.

On the 9th July, 1954, a large area lying to the south and south-west of the Forest Park (see map on front end paper) was declared a nature reserve under the management of the Nature Conservancy Council, 12 Hope Terrace, Edinburgh EH9 2AS. This reserve, the Cairngorms National Nature Reserve, is now the largest in Britain and includes nearly 64 square miles of mountain and forest. The aim of the Nature Conservancy is to preserve the native flora and fauna, but the walking and climbing public, provided they observe the Country Code of good conduct, are welcome within the Reserve, and only under exceptional circumstances will they be requested to avoid for a few weeks in the year certain restricted areas where birds or animals are breeding. The collection of specimens is not allowed without special permission from the Nature Conservancy Council, and then only for scientific purposes.

This large area now comprising both Forest Park and the Cairngorms National Nature Reserve, on which plant and animal life is protected, will undoubtedly help to keep in a vigorous state the wild life in this important and representative part of the Cairngorms, and provide scope for the study of our native plants and animals living in natural conditions. It provides a great variety of habitats ranging from the exposed wind-swept summits with their late-lying snow, to the moorlands and forests at lower altitudes.

Grateful acknowledgment is here made to those who have so willingly co-operated in the production of this Guide, the writers of the chapters dealing with the various aspects of the Park, its inhabitants and its history, the artists whose work adorns its pages, the photographers to whose skill and artistic judgment we owe the fine illustrations, and the local staff of the Forestry Commission, whose detailed knowledge of the district has proved invaluable.

Special thanks are due to the Publications Officer of the Forestry Commission, Mr. H. L. Edlin, whose effective assistance has made the production of this book a pleasant task. The greater part of any success this booklet achieves must be credited to him.

Robin Og and the Fairy Puff Ball

Part of my mind is crossed by twisting highland roads:
over the wilderness of lost generations . . .
it has become a habit not to tempt enemies
or providence with straight Roman access . . .

— Robin Fulton

HISTORY AND TRADITION

By A. Macpherson Grant

For centuries the Privy Council of Scotland maintained the Highlands in a state of submission, keeping them in subjection by repressive measures. Glen More, however, does not appear in their records; either the district was too well-behaved for censure, or else there were no inhabitants. This last is the obvious choice; Glen More meant trees and little else.

But though one cannot refer to clan battles and local traditions in Glen More itself, there is ample history all around it. To the north lay Clan Grant and nearby is Rothiemurchus—home of Grants and Shaws; to the south is Badenoch, crossed and recrossed by forces loyal or revolutionary; to the west was the country of the Clan Chattan, an uneasy confederation of Mackintoshes, Macphersons, MacGillivrays, and a dozen other septs.

The Earls of Huntly, to whom the Government of the district was entrusted by the Crown, divided the land on terms to the local chiefs, who kept a large number of restless adherents on an insufficient acreage of soil. Nominally, these adherents were supposed to uphold the banner of their overlord; in practice they obeyed their chief. It was a system within a system, and feudal in name only. In 1684 the fourth Marquis of Huntly was created Duke of Gordon, and his family continued to own great tracts of land in Strath Spey. At one time their domains extended from sea to sea, from Speymouth to Fort William. Their most important stronghold was the castle of Ruthven near Kingussie, and it is only worthy of such a historical spot that the main road close by should be persistently haunted at night.

Strath Spey is a valley of music, romance, and tradition, but always martial, as witness the annals of the 51st Highland Division. Badenoch was forever the scene of restlessness. Montrose traversed it many times on his unbelievable marches, and in the '45 Prince Charlie's forces, coming from Glenfinnan, consolidated themselves there and enrolled Cluny Macpherson, a local hero, who hid himself for nine years among his native hills, while the royal forces searched for him in vain. Hundreds of people could have located him, but in spite of a princely bribe, none did so. Badenoch prides itself on its nobility to this day.

A still more extraordinary story is that of Mackintosh, chief of his clan, who served through the '45 in the Hanoverian forces, while his wife, young Lady Anne, raised the clan on behalf of Prince Charlie. Mackintosh did not forfeit his estate, and Lady Anne was not hanged, but one wonders how this domestic difference was settled in later years.

Scarcely any of the leading men in Lower Badenoch joined the Jacobite Risings. They remained neutral and in 1715 actually imprisoned in Loch an Eilein Castle one of their number suspected of a desire to join the Hanoverians.

One cannot be long in the district before hearing of Jean, Duchess of Gordon. She raised many recruits for the Gordon Highlanders, but the story that she rode about holding a guinea between her lips and allowing recruits to take hold of it similarly is untrue. She is buried at Kinrara, in the wood near the house, and her grave belongs to the Gordon Highlanders.

Glen More continued in the ownership of the Dukes of Gordon until its acquisition by the Forestry Commissioners in 1923. Let us turn from the study of its past and have a day amongst its trees. Be an animal for the day, and associate yourself with the local animals who really own the place. Let these animals be: it's their country, not yours. Look how a dainty roebuck springs into view and how madam will deceive you as to the whereabouts of her fawn, among the bracken. That rare little bird is the crested tit—but do spare its nest—nor seek the home of the handsome peregrine. Talk of it, and a crowd of people may come out with guns. If you are so lucky as to find that most beautiful and rarest of Highland woodland plants, the *Linnaea borealis*, forget where the plant is, or a platoon of spade-men may come and dig it up.

Going further afield, there are historic sites to be visited in the island castle of Loch an Eilein, the churchyard of Insch beyond Kincraig, and the battlefield of Culloden, which last is easily reached by road from Aviemore. The remains of prehistoric peoples persist in the Picts House just east of Kingussie, and in the stone circles around Aviemore village.

The hills bounding Glen More, nowadays called the Cairngorms or Blue Hills, were formerly known as the Monadh Ruadh (Red-brown Hills) to distinguish them from the hills across the Spey still called the Monadh Liath, or Grey Hills. These don't afford much scenery but offer hill tracks towards Inverness.

There are ruins of shielings in plenty among the Monadh Liath, and here a word as to a shieling. About May every year the women and children were escorted to their temporary shieling homes and there left by the men to their summer task of rearing young animals and butter-making till summer was over. The Highland boys learnt their agility tending young cattle amongst the hills, and were kept occupied unwillingly, in the evening, by learning to knit. *Ruidh* and *airidh* were the common names for shielings.

The loneliness of the women's work found expression in the many touching shieling songs which are the most beautiful in Gaelic poetry. Here is the translation of a passage from one such song:

> "But 'tis pity that I and my sweetheart of flowing locks were not in the little green clump, where the wood pigeon will crow; in the rushy thicket in which would be the roebuck—and the heather around us in dark green folds."

GHOSTS AND FAIRIES

The Cairngorms are traditionally the home of that strange mythical creature known in Gaelic as the *famh* (pronounced "fav", and normally signifying a mole). According to the *Statistical Account of Scotland*, Kirkmichael parish (1794), "In summer mornings it issues from its lurking places, emitting a kind of glutinous matter fatal to horses if they happen to eat the grass upon which it has been deposited. It is somewhat larger than a mole, of a brownish

6

colour, with a large head disproportionate to its body. Other quadrupeds once indigenous to the Grampian Mountains are now extinct, such as the *torc neimh* or wild boar."

James Hogg mentions the "fahm" in his poem *The Queen's Wake*, and the anonymous editor of Chambers's 1841 edition of that work provides the following information:

> "Fahm is a little ugly monster, who frequents the summits of the mountains around Glen Avin, and no other place in the world that I know of. My guide, D. M'Queen, declared that he had himself seen him, and, by his description. Fahm appears to be no native of this world, but an occasional visitant, whose intentions are evil and dangerous. He is only seen about the break of day, and on the highest verge of the mountain. His head is twice as large as his whole body beside; and if any living creature cross the track over which he has passed, before the sun shine upon it, certain death is the consequence."

It is possible that this curious legend arose from the survival into early historic times of some small arctic beast (such as the lemming) that has since become extinct in Scotland.

A more recent discovery is the *Fear Liath Mór* or Great Grey Man, said by certain modern climbers to haunt the summit of Ben Macdui. He is a ghostly figure who follows one with pattering feet. Snow whirls can look surprisingly human at times, and eerie is the sough of the wind in the corrie!

The following explanation of his giant footprints has been advanced by William Morison, Head Forester at Glen More:

> "Under freak atmospheric conditions lumps of ice, formed high in the clouds, fall at regular intervals in a straight line across country. They leave deep imprints in soft snowfields that suggest the passage of a huge striding man."

Fairies are said to dance on moonlight nights around the peculiar little conical hill just above Lochan Uaine. Once a wandering shepherd named Robin Og stole their tiny fairy bagpipes, but when dawn came he found himself holding nothing except a puff ball to which a few blades of grass were attached!

At the Ceilidh

A throwing stone perhaps   its surface carved
to six faces   studs raised from a basic sphere
heavy,   big as a rabbit's head   and fitting to the hand.
Perhaps a sinker   for nets   (there is difference
of opinion on its function)   certain it is very old
and older than roof-beams buried in the peat.
But a stone for killing   is the most likely
so well it fits the hand.   Design to penetrate a life.

- – Roderick Watson

THE OLD WAYS OF LIFE
IN STRATH SPEY

By Miss I. F. Grant

In a sparsely occupied country like the Highlands abundant vestiges may be traced of the people who once lived there, although the appearance of Strath Spey has been altered to some extent by the clearance of some forests and the establishment of others, and there have been similar changes in the location of agricultural land. In the old days the floors of the straths were largely swamps, only useful for cutting the coarse natural grass to serve as winter feeding. Some of this land is once more uncultivated, but old ditches and embankments are reminders of more prosperous days for farming. Of such good times the Napoleonic wars formed a highwater-mark.

8

Means of communication seldom followed the valleys. The old drove roads, mere tracks, generally crossed them and went over the hills. Several can still be traced on the Cairngorms and the Monadh Liath. Raiding clansmen, adventurous packmen, the great droves of cattle that were the Highlanders' main source of wealth and were yearly driven down to the Southern markets, all used them. Two such roads actually cross the Forest Park, one linking Aviemore with Strath Nethy by the Ryvoan Pass, the other—the famous "Caterans' Road"—running from Ryvoan south-westwards along the lower slopes of Cairn Gorm towards Upper Badenoch.

The layout of Highland farms varied according to the configuration of the land, but in the wider straths the townships were generally grouped along the hill slopes (the Gaelic *baile*, township, survives in many place-names beginning with "Bal"). Eight joint-tenants was a convenient number, for each tenant provided a beast, horse or ox, for the team that drew the clumsy wooden plough that tilled all the lands of the township. Regular fields or fences there were none. Patches of the best, and most rock-free land, called the "infield", received all the manure and were kept under constant crops of rye and inferior oats and barley. A proportion of the less suitable land, the "outfield", was cropped in the same way till it was exhausted and then was abandoned for a time. Turnips were not grown and there was no sown hay, so the animals fared badly in the winter. But in the summer the beasts and the people who looked after them had a very happy time, for they went up to the shielings in the sweet hill pastures.

Often still one comes across traces of the old cultivation, patches o narrow, crooked ridges, often on very steep slopes. The old methods gave a very poor return. When the seasons were unfavourable most people went short of food for part of the year. Work was very laborious; corn was threshed with the flail and reaped with the sickle. The new system of separate holdings and regular fields tilled under a rotation of crops, was developed in southern Scotland in the eighteenth century and thence gradually made its way into the Highlands. The making of field drains, which brought much of our best land into cultivation, came later, and tile drainage was only being introduced about a hundred years ago.

In the old days everyone grew a "spot" of flax—often in the large gardens of which one sees traces near old cottages. The people themselves performed the rather unpleasant processes required for preparing the lint, and the women of the household spun the yarn for clothing and household napery, and it was woven by the local weaver. Wool was dyed and spun at home and woven by the weaver into cloth and plaids and blankets. Harness (mostly of wood),

9

baskets and wooden bowls and platters were made at home from local materials. Such things as milk cogs and cruisie lamps were made by the village cooper and blacksmith. The neighbours would unite in building each others' houses, small but warm, and easily added to or repaired because all the materials were found to hand. The tinkers made horn spoons or would hammer a coin into a brooch.

The people's pleasures were also home made. Mrs. Grant of Laggan, writing of the upper valley of the Spey, said that in every cottage there was a musician and in every hamlet a poet. Gathered about the glowing peatfire to spin and carry on their other crafts, the people not only sang old songs and told old tales, but they improvised, wittily if not always charitably. Their great collection of oral traditions about their legendary heroes, the Feine, was constantly being added to, like a serial story. It was at Ruthven, just up the strath, that James Macpherson, the young schoolmaster, learnt the stories on which he based his *Ossian*, which entranced the literary world of the eighteenth century.

It is a strange thing that the work rhythms of these long-dead Highlanders should still survive when so much else has vanished, but our loveliest traditional song-tunes were made to help people through the drudgery of working with the simplest tools. The people lived in an atmosphere of song and their lilt is with us yet.

Anyone who would like to see examples of the old implements and plenishings, of the lovely fabrics and of the other crafts, and how the houses were built and furnished, can visit the most comprehensive collection of its kind in Scotland, *Am Fasgadh*, the Highland Folk Museum at Kingussie, which is open to the public from 1st May to the end of September each year. This museum, first established by Dr. I. F. Grant in 1934, has been acquired by the Highland Regional Council. Their aim is to make it a centre which will not only remind Scotland and her visitors of the origins of materials and customs, but which will become a show place to world students of Highland folklore and antiquities.

There is also a fine collection of Highland antiquities in the Burgh Museum, Inverness.

The Barns of Bynack

The hills
year after year are monotonous
shaded now and again by a drifting cloud
or by an occasional autumn with purple shadows;

For the curious
there are small hard revelations:
Plates of soft shale flake in your fingers
and the whorled fossil is at last unlocked.

— Robin Fulton

GEOLOGY

By Professor J. G. C. Anderson

The Cairngorm Mountains, which include four of the five highest
peaks in the British Isles, and by far the most extensive area over
3,000 feet, form a distinctive part of the Scottish Highlands. Their
individuality is largely a reflection of their geological character,
for the main part of the range has been sculptured from one of the
largest granite masses in the country, with a total outcrop of some
160 square miles.

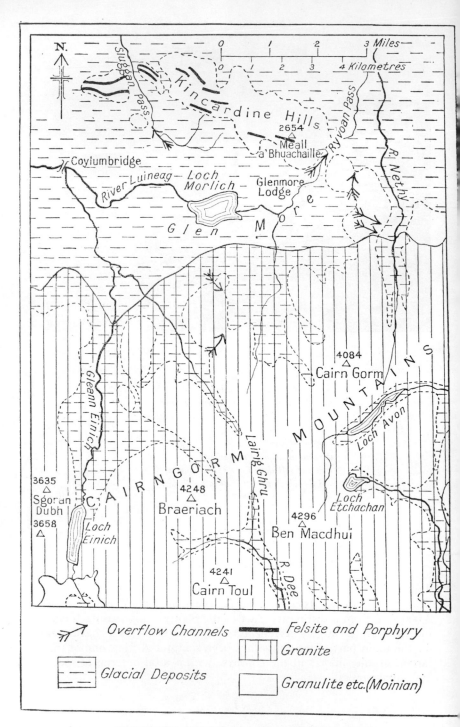

GEOLOGICAL SKETCH MAP OF THE FOREST PARK

It is the prevalence of the granite which gave rise to the old name of the mountains, the Monadh Ruadh or Red Hills—in contrast to the Monadh Liath or Grey Hills on the opposite side of the Spey, which are composed mainly of schist. On the other hand the modern name has passed into mineralogical terminology through being applied to the well-known ornamental stone—a variety of quartz.

Though the Cairngorm granite is of great antiquity—it was formed by the consolidation of molten material in late Silurian or early Devonian times some 300 million years ago—it is by no means the oldest rock of the district, as it was intruded into still more ancient metamorphic rocks, mainly granulites (or psammitic schists as they are sometimes called). The granulites were formed by the metamorphism, or alteration by intense heat and pressure, of sandstones. Interbedded with the granulites are thin layers of mica-schist (sometimes called pelitic schist) produced by the alteration of originally clayey sediments. Igneous rocks other than the granite which occur in the district include irregular veins of pegmatite and sheet-like intrusions of felsite and porphyry.

Throughout most of the lower ground the "solid" rocks mentioned above are hidden under a mantle of unconsolidated superficial or drift deposits, nearly all of which are of glacial origin. The glacial deposits are particularly thick and widespread along the northern side of the Cairngorm Mountains, where their presence has encouraged the growth of the great Rothiemurchus Forest.

THE METAMORPHIC ROCKS

The metamorphic rocks are often spoken of as the Central Highland Granulites, and are grey or pinkish, fine- to medium-grained rocks composed essentially of the minerals quartz and felspar, with scattered flakes of mica. Thin layers, very rich in mica, are present at irregular intervals. Weathering along these gives the granulites a characteristically flaggy appearance.

The Central Highland Granulites form part of the Moinian Assemblage, a major sub-division of the Highland metamorphic strata. Their age is a matter of dispute, but they are almost certainly pre-Cambrian, that is, older than the earliest formation with recognisable fossils.

The granulites, along with other Highland strata, were involved in Silurian times in major horizontal movements of the earth's crust accompanying what is known as the Caledonian Period of mountain building, which brought into existence a great chain, with a general north-easterly trend, in Scotland and Scandinavia. To appreciate the major structures resulting from these disturbances requires the study of a wide area, but the minor effects are seen in the small-scale

13

folding and distortion of the metamorphic strata visible in numerous rock-faces in the district.

PEGMATITE VEINS

Throughout much of the area the granulites are penetrated by thin irregular veins termed pegmatites. These are of the same composition as granite, that is to say they consist of the minerals quartz, felspar and mica, but are much more coarsely crystalline. Most of the pegmatites are earlier than, and unconnected with, the main Cairngorm granite.

THE CAIRNGORM GRANITE

The granite is normally a fairly coarse-grained rock composed of quartz and red felspar with a little mica. Fine-grained varieties also occur in some areas. The granite is usually cut by widely spaced, strongly marked, rectangular joints, weathering along which gives rise to the "mural" or walled appearance characteristic of the precipitous sides of the great corries in the heart of the range.

It is in veins and cavities in the granite that the "cairngorms" occur. The "cairngorm" crystals, which are generally associated with felspar and mica, vary in colour from yellow to black; they are often somewhat smoky. "Cairngorms" are also found as loose crystals in the disintegrated granite debris which covers much of the Cairngorm Plateau, and they occur as pebbles in some of the rivers. The search for "cairngorms" was at one time a profitable industry, but it has been discontinued for many years owing to the import of cheap foreign stones. Beryls are not infrequent in some localities and are known locally as "green cairngorms".

FELSITES AND PORPHYRIES

At some localities in the northern part of the area, thin, sheet-like bodies of igneous rock (technically termed sills) may be seen in the granulites. These are of a pinkish colour and are of the same composition as the granite but much finer in grain. The felsites are even-grained: the porphyries contain scattered large crystals set in a fine-grained matrix.

TOPOGRAPHY

The striking relief of the district is not, as often imagined, the direct result either of the earth movements already mentioned or of the intrusion of the granite. The scenery, as is the case throughout the Highlands, is the result of sculpture. The Cairngorm Mountains are portions of a high plateau deeply dissected by river valleys.

The slope of the primitive Highland plateau as a whole was south-easterly and the original rivers followed this direction. The Lairig Ghru is a relic of one of these "consequent" valleys, as they are termed. As time went on so the "consequent" valleys were inter-sected by north-easterly flowing "subsequent" rivers, following the old north-easterly "grain" of the country, of which the Spey is a notable example.

The evolution of the broad topographic features was complete before the glacial epoch, but erosion by ice was responsible for modifications such as the formation of corries and of broad U-shaped valleys. Many minor details of the landscape, too, are due either to glacial action or to the presence of glacial deposits.

GLACIATION

The glacial history of the region is complex, and in the present account it is possible to indicate only its salient features. At one time it is probable that the whole of the Cairngorms was covered by a great ice-sheet. As far as the district around Loch Morlich is con-cerned, however, chief interest attached to a later stage during which the higher Cairngorms were mostly free from ice, while Glen More was occupied by a great lobe of ice branching off a major glacier coming down the Spey valley. The Glen More glacier, as it may be termed, was responsible for the deposition of most, if not all, of the glacial deposits of the district. Proof of this statement lies in the fact that the majority of the stones in these glacial deposits consist of various types of schist; if ice from the Cairngorms had been respon-sible, granite should have predominated.

The glacial deposits are of various types. Lateral moraines deposited along the margins of the Glen More glacier form an almost continuous series of low ridges, for the most part at between the 1,500 and the 2,000 feet levels, along the northern slopes of the Cairngorms and the southern slopes of the Kincardine Hills. Ground moraine, formed under the ice, is represented by the com-paratively smooth sheet of clayey drift which covers the southern slope of the Kincardine Hills.

By far the most widespread glacial deposits of the district, how-ever, are the gravelly morainic deposits which floor most of the low ground. These have a typical moundy or hummocky form and consist of a rather ill-assorted mixture of sand, gravel and clay. They were deposited at the ice front during various stages of retreat of the ice.

At its maximum the Glen More ice escaped northwards through the Ryvoan Pass. Successive pauses in its retreat southwards through the pass are indicated by the moraines which cross the glen at intervals. Above each of these lies a peaty flat marking the site of a small tarn held up for a time by the moraine below. The green waters of An Lochan Uaine still occupy the highest of these ponded lochans.

Loch Morlich itself is a large "kettle-hole", a hollow left on the final melting of a great block of ice—possibly a last remnant of the stagnant Glen More glacier. Other deposits, differing in character from moraines and termed "fluvioglacial", form very extensive terraces in Gleann Einich and smaller terraces at the northern entrance to the Lairig Ghru. They were deposited by running water in temporary lochs brought into being when tongues of the Glen More glacier dammed the valleys in which they lie.

The blockage of the normal drainage by the ice also had the effect of diverting the water through various overflow channels which on the disappearance of the ice were left as dry valleys or gullies. Several of these overflow channels, for instance, breach the ridge of Stac na h'Iolaire east of Glen More Lodge, and were formed when ice forced the water draining from the northern slopes of Cairn Gorm to escape eastwards into Strath Nethy. Another forms a conspicuous notch in the ridge of Creag a' Chalamain, on the east side of the stream draining northwards from the Lairig Ghru. At one stage, too, the Sluggan pass functioned as an overflow channel. (See sketch map on page 12).

POST-GLACIAL DEPOSITS

The alluvial terraces along the course of many of the streams, and the peat covering parts of the flatter ground, are examples of deposits formed after the disappearance of the ice. Comparatively recent deposits which contribute to the beauty of the district are the sandy beaches of Loch Morlich and the sand dunes at its eastern end.

BIBLIOGRAPHY

The geology of the National Forest Park area is shown on sheet 74 of the 1-inch to the mile Geological Map of Scotland; the Cairngorm Mountains as a whole are shown on sheets 64, 65, 74 and 75.

Geological Survey Memoirs dealing with parts of the Cairngorm Mountains are:

BARROW, G. and others — 1912: *The Geology of the Districts of Braemar, Ballater and Glen Clova* (explanation of Sheet 65)

BARROW, G. and others — 1913: *The Geology of Upper Strathspey, Gaick and the Forest of Atholl* (explanation of Sheet 64)

HINXMAN, L. W. — 1896: *West Aberdeenshire, Banffshire, parts of Elgin and Inverness* (explanation of Sheet 75)

HINXMAN, L. W. and others — 1915: *The Geology of Mid-Strathspey and Strathdearn* (explanation of Sheet 74)

READ, H. H. and A. G. MACGREGOR — 1948: *British Regional Geology: The Grampian Highlands* (2nd Edition)

The Approach to Loch Morlich

Pink sand and sandpipers pink in the setting
sun and pink granite and the pink swirl
of green waves; no Mediterranean relics
here, no ruined amphitheatres, no amphorae,

no half-submerged statuary — only the
children's wet sand-pies.

— Tom Buchan

LOCH MORLICH

By R. Brown and P. E. O'Sullivan

A central feature of Glenmore is Loch Morlich, which, in terms of surface area, is the largest of the Speyside lochs. The loch measures 1.6 by 1 km (roughly one mile long by two-thirds of a mile across), and has a maximum depth of 14.5 metres (47 feeet) close to the eastern shore. The surface of the water lies at 335 metres (1,100 feet) above sea-level, although the drainage basin of Loch Morlich, which includes the north slope of the Cairngorm range, extends to over 1,200 metres (4,000 feet) encompassing some of the highest land in Scotland, as shown by the maps in this guide book. The following article summarises the results of several years' investigation in and

17

around Glenmore, mainly by parties of undergraduate students. Whilst the authors therefore acknowledge the limitations of some aspects of the work, they nonetheless feel that it contains some information which the general visitor will find interesting.

A detailed bathymetric survey, undertaken in 1974 by an expedition from West Park Secondary School, South Shields, County Durham, demonstrates the sublacustrine topography of the loch (Figure 1). Most of the loch is relatively shallow, being less than 10 metres deep, and shelves gently from west to east. At the eastern end, however, close to the Forest Park camp site, there is a deeper basin, reaching over 12 metres (40 feet) in depth, with a very steep slope offshore. The results of this survey are consistent with the theory of the origin of Loch Morlich, which is that it is a kettle-hole formed at the end of the ice-age, and later flooded due to the damming action of the morainic deposit west of the loch. In this case, the deep eastern basin corresponds to the kettle-hole.

The sublacustrine shape, or morphometry, of Loch Morlich is important, in that at certain times of the year it controls the temperature structure of the loch. Readings of water temperature taken in April 1974 (Figure 2, top) show that a body of colder, denser water at about 7 degs. C occupied the deepest part of the loch, whilst the shallower areas consisted of warmer, and therefore lighter water at about 10 degs. C. This phenomenon, known as thermal stratification, is a well-recognised feature of many lakes throughout temperate latitudes, and an important factor controlling aspects of their physical and biological regime, mainly because of the inability of the cold, dense water to mix with the lighter layers above

Measurements of the oxygen concentration in the water, taken at the same time as the temperature measurements, illustrate the segregation of the upper and lower waters during stratification In the upper parts of the lake, oxygen levels were at 82% saturation, whilst in the deeper parts of the lake they fell below 70% saturation.

By October 1974, the stratification had broken down, and the loch had become broadly isothermal, with a surface temperature of 8.2 degs. C, and a temperature of 7.8 degs. C at 14 metres depth. Oxygen levels were constant at 72–74% saturation at all depths (Figure 2, bottom).

These results are explicable in terms of the behaviour of water bodies in response to seasonal temperature and other climatic changes. Warming up of lake waters in the spring creates a layer of warmer, less dense water near the surface (*epilimnion*), whilst the colder, denser layers remain at the bottom of the lake (*hypolimnion*).

LOCH MORLICH

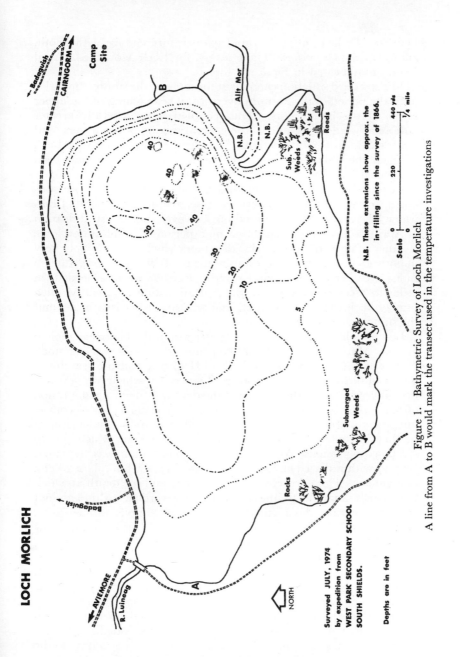

Surveyed JULY, 1974
by expedition from
WEST PARK SECONDARY SCHOOL
SOUTH SHIELDS.

Depths are in feet

NORTH

N.B. These extensions show approx. the
in-filling since the survey of 1866.

Scale

0   220   440 yds

0   ¼ mile

Figure 1. Bathymetric Survey of Loch Morlich
A line from A to B would mark the transect used in the temperature investigations

19

Between is a layer of fairly rapid temperature change with depth, known as the *thermocline*. These layers, for Loch Morlich, in April 1974, are indicated in Figure 2, top.

The stratified situation can persist throughout the summer months, until the period of the autumn overturn, when cooling of the upper layers of the lake occurs. This, coupled with generally greater autumnal windspeeds, allows the general mixing of the waters, and the breakdown of stratification. The October 1974 results for Loch Morlich show that by this time, the autumn overturn had been completed, and the summer stratification broken down.

In terms of its physical limnology, Loch Morlich therefore conforms to a well-established pattern of behaviour in temperate freshwater lakes. It must be pointed out however that the stratification of April 1974 was observed following a period of calm, anticyclonic weather of at least three weeks' duration, which was probably very important in allowing the establishment of the *epilimnion*, due to sunny weather and low wind speeds. Further work is needed, in order to ascertain whether summer stratification in Loch Morlich usually begins later in the year, and whether it persists throughout the summer.

Less data has so far been accumulated about the biological regime of Loch Morlich. The chemical content of the water was examined by Gorham (1957), who reported a pH of 6.4, and the scarcity of dissolved nitrogen and phosphorus. One aspect which has however been investigated by the authors is the depth of effective penetration of light into the water of the loch. This parameter is, of course, important to the plant life of the loch, both macro- and microscopic, in that it controls the depth of water throughout which photosynthesis is possible. Average depth of penetration was measured simply, with a device known as a Secchi disc, a white plate 20 cm. in diameter. This is lowered into the water, and the depth at which it becomes invisible to the human eye recorded. Although not entirely accurate, this method is a relatively simple, rapid way of estimating the depth of the *photic zone* in any lake. The results show that in April 1974, the average depth of penetration was 4 metres, whilst by October 1974, this had been reduced to 3 metres depth. During stratification, photosynthesis is thus confined to the *epilimnion*, which is probably an important factor in maintaining oxygen levels in the upper layers. The October readings illustrate the generally more turbid character of lake waters following the autumn overturn, during which fine sediments are often resuspended.

Some investigations have also been made into the nature of the bottom sediments of Loch Morlich. Around the shores, a basically sandy or stony bottom to the loch is found, but in the deeper parts,

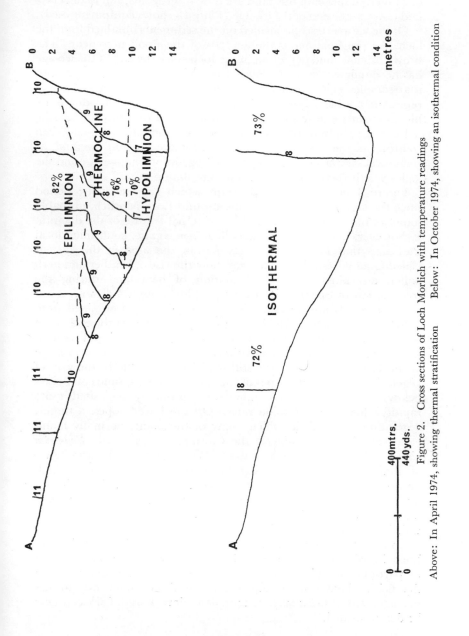

Figure 2.   Cross sections of Loch Morlich with temperature readings

Above: In April 1974, showing thermal stratification   Below: In October 1974, showing an isothermal condition

21

this gives way to a fine brown, organic mud, with an average depth of 2½ metres. Beneath this mud are pink or grey silts, sands and clays laid down at the end of the ice-age (Plate 18 shows equipment used).

Of the various tests performed on the sediments obtained from the loch, the principal one is the analysis of their pollen content. The brown organic mud deposited in the loch since the end of the ice-age has accumulated gradually over a period of up to 10,000 years, so that samples taken vertically throughout the mud can be said to represent a time sequence. The pollen and spores produced by higher plants are very durable, and are incorporated in lake sediments in substantial numbers, so that identification and then counting of the various pollen types preserved within the mud, at each level sampled, gives a picture of vegetation changes around the loch over the period of sediment accumulation.

Figure 3 shows a pollen diagram which represents the period since the establishment of the alder around Loch Morlich, probably some six thousand years ago. The principal feature of the diagram is, however, that the main tree pollen type is pine, confirming local traditions that Loch Morlich lay within the area of the ancient Caledonian Forest. Later changes show the rise of heather and herb pollen associated with the formation of heathland during the colonisation of Speyside by Celtic peoples around 400 A.D.

These results are consistent with pollen diagrams obtained from other lakes in the Speyside district which show that at the end of the ice-age, a basically treeless landscape was to be found around Glenmore. Presumably at this time, the corries on the north slope of the Cairngorms may have still held ice, and little in the way of vegetation covered the slopes of the hills. The silts, sands and clays below the brown organic mud were probably deposited quite rapidly, due to high erosion rates. On the lower slopes, a tundra vegetation persisted, in which many of the plants normally found today at higher altitudes in the Cairngorms, especially *Empetrum nigrum* (crowberry), were abundant. With the gradual warming up of climate, the tundra was progressively replaced by scrub, in which juniper was prominent, and later, deciduous woodland dominated by birch, rowan and aspen. Some time after 8,000 years ago, this woodland was colonised by the pine, and the original form of the Caledonian Forest established.

Apart from the pollen-analytical work, these investigations in Loch Morlich illustrate the kind of results which can be obtained by parties of school or college students under careful supervision in the field. That such results can have direct relevance to the management of areas such as the Glen More Forest Park can now be demonstrated.

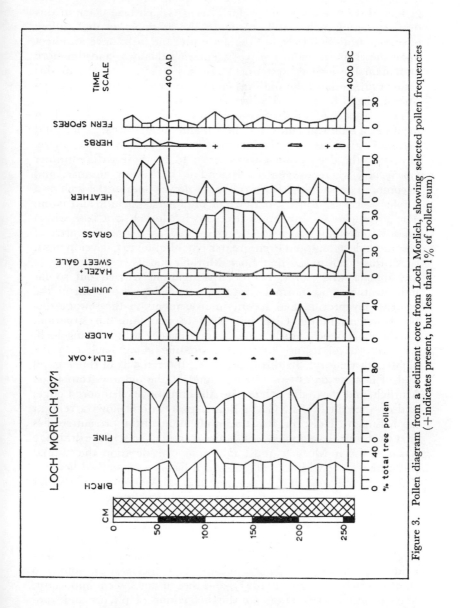

Figure 3. Pollen diagram from a sediment core from Loch Morlich, showing selected pollen frequencies (+indicates present, but less than 1% of pollen sum)

23

As shown on the maps, the area drained by the loch consists both of the main areas given over to development in the bottom of the glen, and the ski-slopes. Therefore, events which take place in this drainage basin, such as soil erosion on the ski-slopes, or the outflow of sewage from buildings in Glenmore into the loch, have an effect upon the chemical nature of water entering the loch, and therefore also upon the loch ecosystem. More important, however, in this context are perhaps the findings concerning the internal character-istics of the loch described above.

The existence of a deep basin offshore at the east end of the loch means that sediment tends to collect mainly in this area. Thus solid material introduced into the loch may eventually find its way there. However, the deep basin happens also to be the area of summer *hypolimnion*, where oxygen levels tend to be low in summer, and decomposition rates therefore probably slower than in the loch as a whole, especially during periods of prolonged warmth and calm. The investigations thus imply that Loch Morlich is a lake which must be carefully managed, being located as it is in an area of considerable actual, and even greater potential tourist, development.

All this is not to say that Loch Morlich and its ecosystem are in any danger whatsoever. Those investigations carried out so far indicate that quite normal conditions for a lake ecosystem at the present day prevail, and recent improvements in the sewage dis-posal systems in the Glen will help to maintain this situation. Furthermore, Loch Morlich has a long history as a working loch, with records of its use for timber floating going back into the eighteenth century. In this connection, the remains of sluice gates and of floating dams can still be found at the outflow from Loch Morlich, and above the loch on the Allt Ban above Glenmore Lodge, and on the Allt Mor at Clach Bharraig. (Plate 6 shows a relic at Loch Einich). However, it is the implication of the present studies that the future development of Glenmore, and the rest of the drainage basin of Loch Morlich, must take into consideration the annual physical regime within the loch, which has been described here.

Many more areas of investigation in Loch Morlich remain so far unexplored. For example the temperature structure of the loch at midsummer and midwinter have not yet been examined. It is known that the loch freezes in part in most winters, but it is thought that only in hard winters such as 1949–50, 1950–51 and 1962–63, is freezing-over totally achieved. Similarly, in the light of the present evidence, data on the chemical nature of the loch waters, similar to that collected by Gorham (1957), and their inflows, seem important, as does some information on the behaviour of phyto- and zoo-plankton populations in the loch throughout the year. Future work

24

Plate 1. Old natural pine forest above Ryvoan Pass.

Plate 2. Looking down Ryvoan Pass to the Green Lochan. The far snow-wreathed hollow is Coire an Lochan, the notch in the hills marks the Creag a' Chalamain.

Plate 3. Loch Morlich in winter, looking towards Coire Cas.

Plate 4. Cairngorm seen from Loch Morlich at the outlet of the River Luincag.

Plate 5. Loch Morlich and the Monadhliaths seen from the Ski Road. A glacial moraine, now undergoing erosion, occupies the foreground.

Plate 6. The remains of the last timber-floating dam, at the outlet of Loch Einich.

Plate 7.   The moraine-dammed lochan in the Coire an Lochan.

Plate 8.   The glacial overflow channel below Creag a' Chalamain.

Plate 9. Loch Morlich beach in spring.

Plate 10. Water sports on Loch Morlich.

Plate 11. Avalanche in the Coire an Lochan.

Plate 12.   Near view of the head of the avalanche in the Coire an Lochan.

Plate 13.   Fishing at the outlet of the Allt Mor.

Plate 14.   Beachcombing.

thus lies in these directions. Meanwhile, the authors hope that this description of some aspects of Loch Morlich, and its annual changes, will be of use to all who wish to enjoy the many pleasures that the loch affords.

ACKNOWLEDGEMENTS

The authors are grateful to the Conservator of Forests for North Scotland, Inverness, for permission to work on Loch Morlich, and to Mr. William Morison, Chief Forester at Glenmore, for his considerable help on the ground. They are also anxious to acknowledge the labour and enthusiams of the several parties of students who have now helped them with their studies of Loch Morlich.

SUGGESTED FURTHER READING

CASH, C. G.	1905: Timber-floating at Rothiemurchus. *Cairngorm Club Journal.* 4 : 301
GORHAM, E.	1957: The chemical composition of some natural lake waters in the Strath Spey-Cairngorm district of Scotland. *Limnology and Oceanography.* 2 : 143–155
GRANT, E.	1898: *Memoirs of a Highland Lady (1797–1827)*: ed. Lady Strachey. London
MACAN, T. T.	1970: *Biological Studies of the English Lakes.* Longmans
MACAN, T. T. and WORTHINGTON, E. G.	1972: *Life in Lakes and Rivers.* Collins New Naturalist (rev. edn)
O'SULLIVAN, P. E.	1975: *Environmental History of the Speyside District of the Cairngorm Mountains, Scotland* (in prep.)
WEIR, T.	1970: *The Scottish Lochs* (Vol. 1). Constable (254 pp.)

R. G. H. Brown is Research Assistant in Geography; and
P. E. O'Sullivan is Lecturer in Geography, Faculty of Humanities, The Polytechnic, Wolverhampton.

Globe Flower

But mostly to the visiting eye of contemplation
A rich harvest may be gleaned from our forest—
Pines of strength, armoured with the antiquity of eagles,
Roarers in the storm, and in the calms
The abode of golden-plumaged and responsive peace;
— William Jeffrey

THE PLANT LIFE
OF THE PARK

By Professor John Walton

To those who take an interest in wild plants the Glen More Forest Park offers an almost inexhaustible supply of subjects for study and delight. Here they will find a magnificent display of mountain vegetation ranging from the pine forests to the arctic-alpine flora of the summits. Large areas of the mountain-sides bear an abundance of plants which occur in only relatively small and scattered patches on other British mountains. Compared with some other Scottish mountains, there are perhaps fewer of the specially rare alpine species. This is no doubt due to differences in climate and chemical composition of the rocks.

Mountain plants have always had a special attraction for those interested in botanical matters. This is in part due to the fact that many of them are found in relatively inaccessible places and then only after considerable bodily exertion. An arduous climb may be amply rewarded by such unforgettable visions as cushions of moss campion (*Silene acaulis*) covered with its brilliant pink blossoms contrasting gloriously with the inhospitable stony places in which it grows at high altitudes, or of the starry saxifrage (*Saxifraga stellaris*). The plants which grow on the exposed hill slopes and at high altitudes appear dwarfed or stunted, but in contrast to this many of them when they flower do so very profusely and may make a most conspicuous display. Several species which are found at these high altitudes are relics of the arctic flora which existed in Britain during the Ice Age, and a flora with many of the same species is found in countries of the far North, e.g., Northern Canada, Greenland, Spitsbergen, and Novaya Zemlya. In these countries we find the moss campion and dwarf willow abundant at sea level. We suppose that when the Ice Age passed away and lower-lying areas acquired a temperate climate, these arctic plants which were inhabitants of the lower-lying ice-free areas, persisted on the higher summits where the conditions most nearly approximate to those found in the Arctic today, and where they had not to compete with plants suited to warmer conditions.

The Glen More Forest Park includes the northern slopes and corries of the Cairn Gorm, Cairn Lochan and Creag an Leth-choin ridge, the strath drained by the Luineag river and the southern slopes of the ridge of mountains (the Kincardine Hills) that runs north-west from the Ryvoan Pass to the Sluggan Pass. Practically the whole of this area is over 1,000 feet above sea level, but owing to the shelter provided by the mountains the limit of tree growth is considerably higher than in most parts of Scotland. Indeed the plantations extend to over 1,500 feet and scattered groups of trees may be found at even higher altitudes. The forest and plantations are mainly situated on areas which have a covering of glacial deposits which provide a deep enough hold for the tree roots. In a few level places on the slope at about 2,000 feet, there are small accumulations of peat in which there may be seen buried stumps of pine, clear evidence that at one time the forests extended to a considerably greater altitude up the mountain sides than they do today. Relics of forests now buried in the peat are found in several parts of Scotland where no forests exist today. The most extensive is on the Moor of Rannoch, where exposed tree stumps may be seen where the main road runs through cuttings in the peat moor.

This eastern part of the Scottish Highlands has a smaller annual rainfall than the westerly part: probably less than two-thirds of that to which the Argyll Forest Park is subject. It is also colder in the winter. The main mass of the Cairngorms consist of granites and felsite while the West Highlands including the Argyll Park consist principally of schists and gneisses.

These differences in climate and geological composition determine very largely the differences we observe between the floras and vegetation of the two regions. In the Argyll Park there are large areas of wet, boggy moorland on peat whereas in the Glen More Park the drier conditions favour a greater proportion of heathland. There is, on account of the greater general altitude and smaller rainfall, less luxuriant growth of mosses and liverworts in the Glen More Park than in the Argyll Park.

The vegetation of the park may be divided into several regions: the aquatic and semi-aquatic vegetation of the loch and its shore, the meadowland, the forests, the open hillsides, moorland, the corries, and the vegetation of the summits.

Loch Morlich, which lies in the centre of the park, is shallow and is not more than about 40 feet deep at its deepest part. At the east end of the loch there is a sandy beach which is practically bare of vegetation except for a few pines and some tussocks of marram grass, here at its maximum height above sea level in Britain. The prevalent west wind blows up the loch and the sandy beach has been formed by wind and wave action. The northern shore shelves very gently and there is a stretch of stones and small boulders which is covered by the loch waters after heavy rainfall. The western end of the loch tends to be muddy. There are few submerged aquatic plants; the water lobelia may be seen with its pale blue-flowered inflorescence projecting above the surface of the water. On all stony shores we find the shore weed (*Littorella uniflora*), the lesser spearwort, *Lycopodium inundatum* and *Hammarbya paludosa*. Alders, willows and pines are found growing on or close to the shore and along the banks of the burn; at least two species of bladderwort (*Utricularia*) are to be found in the muddy shallows at the west end of the loch.

The meadowland extends from the head of the loch eastwards to the lower slopes of Mam Suim. It is a lush grassland with sedges and rushes in the moister areas. Parts of it have been cultivated and used for pasture.

The slightly higher better-drained ground bears forest. There are still considerable areas in the Park in an almost natural state, with wide spaces between the trees which are of different sizes and ages; here we find a rich ground flora of small shrubby plants. The Scots pine (*Pinus sylvestris*) is the principal native tree and is the dominant woodland tree in this region. Some botanists regard the form found in this area as a distinct variety. It differs in some respects from the types of Scots pine found elsewhere in Britain. There is little doubt

28

that pine forest has persisted here ever since the close of the Ice Age. Birches and occasional junipers occur among the pines and with them we find heather or ling (*Calluna vulgaris*), blaeberry (*Vaccinium myrtillus*) and cowberry (*Vaccinium vitis-idaea*) all of which are in the form of small shrubs. We occasionally come across serrate winter-green (*Pyrola media*), *Moneses uniflora*, chickweed-wintergreen (*Trientalis*), and *Linnaea borealis*.

On the slopes of the mountains where there are no woodlands or plantations, and in the small glens, there are occasional trees of pine, birch and rowan, and bushes of juniper and cowberry are abundant, but blaeberry, bell heather (*Erica cinerea*), bearberry (*Arctostaphylos*) and the petty whin (*Genista anglica*) also occur. In the shelter provided by these larger plants we may find the lesser twayblade (*Listera cordata*) and in the more sheltered places on peaty soil the cloudberry (*Rubus chamaemorus*). Where the surface is wind-swept, bearberry, crowberry (*Empetrum nigrum*), and stunted plants of ling and bell heather are predominant, with occasionally *Lyco-podium alpinum* and cat's ear (*Antennaria dioica*).

Several of these plants produce edible berries which may provide welcome refreshment on a hot summer day. The best is the blaeberry (bilberry or whortleberry), which is particularly abundant in the open woodland along the sides of the Allt Mor burn by the path from the Glen More Lodge to Cairn Gorm. The berries are bluish black with a distinct bloom. The crowberry (*Empetrum*) has almost black shiny berries which are rather tasteless, but the juice they provide is refreshing. When cooked they produce a deep purple juice. The cowberry with bright red berries (*Vaccinium vitis-idaea*), sometimes called the Scots cranberry, makes excellent cranberry jam but is not palatable raw. The cloudberry (*Rubus chamaemorus*) has fruits of a pale peach colour when ripe. These are very good eating, but they are not present in any considerable quantity in the Park.

In wet boggy areas along the sides of the burns there are the cross-leaved heath (*Erica tetralix*), bog asphodel, spotted orchis, butterwort and sundew.

Between 2,500 feet and 3,000 feet above sea level the slopes are drier and stony and have no continuous covering of vegetation. The plants are all stunted or lie very close to the ground. Here we find little prostrate shrubs of *Loiseleuria procumbens*, a close relative of our cultivated azaleas. It has small evergreen leaves like a heath and the plants may be covered with very small rose-coloured flowers in late spring. Along with it we may find cushions of moss campion with their bright pink flowers, *Lycopodium selago*, and the very small rush *Juncus trifidus*. In sheltered depressions there may be alpine lady's mantle (*Alchemilla alpina*), bog vaccinium (*V.*

uliginosum) and dwarf cornel (*Chamaepericlymenum suecium*), which has four large petal-like bracts surrounding a group of very small dark-coloured flowers producing a bunch of scarlet berries in the late summer (Plate 17). Lichens and small mosses are abundant.

Above 3,000 feet the vegetation becomes sparser with occasional low cushions of moss campion, the rush *Juncus trifidus*, crowberry and the dwarf or least willow (*Salix herbacea*). The latter although a true willow would hardly be recognized as such by the uninitiated, for its twigs rise but an inch or two from the ground. In August when the catkins are in fruit, the hairy seeds which they release make the plant look as if someone had spread a thin layer of cotton wool over it. In the corries where shelter is greater, there is an admixture of plants which occur elsewhere at lower altitudes, with those which are found high up. For example the globe-flower (*Trollius*) occurs in wet regions on stream banks in the bottoms of the corries, but it is also found elsewhere in Scotland as a plant of wet meadowland.

We find occasional specimens of *Saussaurea alpina* and Scotch asphodel (*Tofieldia pusilla*). On the rock ledges are various species of saxifrage, *Polygonum viviparum* and many mosses and liverworts peculiar to high altitudes.

In a few places above 3,000 feet snow may lie all the year round, and on the ground which is covered with snow late on into the early summer we find a characteristic assemblage of small plants such as *Gnaphalium supinum*, with mosses and liverworts.

This beautiful and interesting stretch of the Scottish Highlands is now open to the public in greater numbers than ever. In the winter when the ground is under snow the plants are safe, but in the summer the chair lifts will bring many more visitors. It is to be hoped that all who visit it will do all they can to help in preserving its natural treasures. In particular visitors should not pick flowers which they discover and above all should not remove any plants. Many of the specially interesting and characteristic mountain plants are just managing to hold their own, and no more, in the struggle for existence, and if man's interference is put in the balance against them they will soon become extinct in the Park.

BIBLIOGRAPHY

The Ecology of the Cairngorms:

WATT, A. S. and JONES, E. W.   1948: Part I: The environment and the altitudinal zonation of the Vegetation. *Journ. of Ecology*, vol. 36, pp. 283–304

METCALFE, G.   1950: Part II: The Mountain Callunetum. *Journ. of Ecology*, vol. 38, pp. 46–74

BURGES, A.   1951: Part III: The Empetrum-Vaccinium Zone. *Journ. of Ecology*, vol. 39, pp. 271–284

General:

TANSLEY, SIR ARTHUR   1939: *The British Islands and their Vegetation.* Cambridge

Ptarmigan in Winter Plumage

The hearth and ploughs of men touch but the fringe of our forest,
The seamew follows no furrow in its midst.
There the curlew and the snipe ply their lonely orchestrations,
The grouse and the raven dwell,
And the eagle from his planetary gyre sinks his shadow deep in light.
— William Jeffrey

THE WILD LIFE OF
GLEN MORE

By Roy H. Dennis

STRATH SPEY and the Cairngorm mountains are one of the finest areas in the British Isles for the naturalist. Here we find in one locality a great diversity of natural habitats ranging from the extensive Scots pine forests of the valley floor, up through the moorland zone to the wild mountain plateaux—the most extensive area of land over 3,000 feet in Britain. This wonderful range of scenery, vegetation, altitude and climate within easy reach of Glen More gives us a rich variety of birds and animals, some of them special to the area.

Standing at the edge of Loch Morlich, 1,100 feet above sea level

31

and thirty miles from the Moray Firth, one could—with luck—see many wonderful sights in the animal world. An osprey or fish-hawk hovering over the still waters of the loch in search of a fish for its young; a family of crested tits noisily searching the bark and foliage of an old Scots pine for insects; a brilliant red cock Scottish crossbill singing from a tree top; a distant eagle winging across the skyline of the Kincardine Hills or a roe deer with her twins drinking at the water's edge. It is all happening as we look out across the loch, over the forest and the gently sloping moors, to the summit of Cairngorm three thousand feet above us. But, alas, our eyes are not as keen as the eagle and we miss most of the inhabitants of the forest; if only we knew how many were watching our progress—possibly a wildcat crouched in the juniper scrub or a peregrine falcon perched high on a rocky pinnacle.

The animal life of Glen More has changed dramatically from the days when elk, bear, wild boar and wolf roamed the old Caledonian Forests. Even in the last few decades there have been noticeable changes in the bird life. In the late 1930s Loch Morlich was remote and few bird-watchers visited its shores; one of the lucky ones discovered the first ever nest of the tiny Temminck's stint in this country. Even fifteen years ago, oyster catchers and ringed plovers nested on the sandy shores of Loch Morlich, now their beach is taken by increasing numbers of holiday-makers.

Nevertheless, there are still many animals and birds in and around the Forest Park. Chaffinches and black-headed gulls walk around us at the car parks and picnic sites searching for scraps, but most of the animals and birds will not come to us, they are shy and will seek cover. To see some of them we will have to work hard and it is important to be as quiet as possible when out looking for them. Roads, forest rides, fire-breaks or paths through the woodland or beside water give the best chance of observing birds and animals. It is well worth stopping or sitting down every now and then to listen for bird calls or watch for movement. Search from vantage points with your binoculars. Early mornings and evening are the best times to see wild life—a walk through the forest not long after dawn on a fine summer's morning can be unforgettable and well worth the effort of getting up at four a.m.!

BIRDS

The bird life of the Forest Park and its surroundings is varied and very interesting; something like one hundred species of birds occur in Glen More annually and about three-quarters of these will nest. Many more species are present in summer than in winter, and because of the very harsh winter conditions quite a few species, which we regard as residents in the lowlands, have to leave the high glens for the winter.

On Loch Morlich, we can observe quite a variety of water birds at times. Very rarely, passing red-throated or black-throated divers will visit the loch and in 1934 a pair of the latter attempted to breed on its shores. Mallard, teal and wigeon are regular and all of them breed in the glen; numbers are usually small but there were, for example twenty-seven wigeon on 16 October 1972. Diving ducks may be represented by tufted duck, pochard, goosander, goldeneye and red-breasted merganser. A few pairs of tree-hole-nesting goosanders are the only regular breeders but tufted duck and mergansers nest nearby. Pochard visit the loch, mainly in late summer and autumn when the flock may sometimes reach forty or fifty birds. Goldeneye are plentiful winter visitors to Strathspey and up to fifty of these beautiful ducks have been seen on Morlich. Most depart for Scandinavia in April and early May but in the last few years a few pairs have remained to nest in Inverness-shire—a new Scottish breeding bird which has taken to nesting in large nest-boxes erected for them beside Highland lochs by the Royal Society for the Protection of Birds. If you find nest-boxes on your walks, please do not look inside as you will frighten the sitting birds and the eggs may be deserted. The goldeneye ducklings are tiny black and white balls of fluff and as soon as they have all hatched the mother duck entices them all to jump out of the nest hole and they fall safely from quite a height on to the water or ground below.

In winter, whooper swans from Iceland occasionally visit the loch to graze on aquatic plants; sometimes coot come to the loch for the same purpose. Migrating grey geese, usually pinkfeet or greylags, quite often pass over the mountains in spring and autumn; in August 1973 a flock of Canada geese were seen flying through Glen More on their way back to Yorkshire from the Beauly Firth, where they moult.

It is one of the greatest thrills to see a golden eagle and one may be very lucky to see an eagle flying over the surrounding hills or even possibly sailing high over the forest. Unfortunately eagles do not like people and one of the disappointing effects of the great increase in visitors into the Cairngorms has been disturbance to some rare birds, in fact some traditional eyries have been deserted. The eagle is a shy bird and will slink off its nest when people approach the nest cliff and will not return until everyone has left the area.

Golden eagles build very large nests or eyries; most eyries in Scotland are in cliffs but some are built in large trees. Each pair usually has several traditional eyries in their territory and each spring one of them is refurbished with sticks and heather, and relined with soft vegetation like wood rush. Two eggs are usually laid but quite often only one youngster is reared. The eggs are incubated for about six weeks and the young fly when about eleven weeks old. This is a long breeding season and if the birds are disturbed when the eggs are in the nest they might easily desert the eyrie or the eggs may be chilled and will not hatch. The food consists mainly of rabbits and mountain hares, ptarmigan and grouse, but even red squirrels and hooded crows are brought to the nest as food for the young.

Buzzards soaring on broad wings can sometimes be confused with golden eagles but the buzzard is smaller and has a faster wing beat. It is more often seen over woodlands or in the valley floor where it nests in woods or cliffs. Buzzards are quite often to be seen perched on telephone posts by the roadside—a favourite vantage point for this opportunist feeder which will eat carrion such as hares killed on the road by cars, young rabbits, moles and even worms. Numbers in Strathspey are now much higher than in the past when they were much persecuted by game-keepers.

Loch Garten and the Royal Society for the Protection of Birds osprey reserve is just over the mountain ridge from Glen More so it is not surprising that ospreys are occasionally seen fishing in Loch Morlich. Long ago a pair used to nest beside the loch but the eggs were stolen by nineteenth-century egg collectors. Since 1959 a pair has nested successfully near Loch Garten—thirty young have now been reared from there over the years. The ospreys return each year from Africa in the first days of April; the nest is rebuilt and two or three beautiful red-brown eggs are laid. Incubation is thirty-five days and the young are about eight weeks when they fly; the birds feed on pike and trout and after the young birds learn to fish in August, they all migrate to the south in September. The ospreys can be viewed at Loch Garten from the Royal Society for the Protection of Birds observation post.

Peregrine falcons, merlins, kestrels and sparrowhawks can be seen in the glen. The sparrowhawks nest in the big woods and feed mainly on small woodland birds. Kestrels mainly haunt the lower ground and are to be seen hovering over forest clearings and open ground in search of mice and voles, although I have seen young birds in late summer hunting on the high plateaux. Merlins and peregrines are much rarer; they are swift of flight and tend to be seen over moorland areas.

The grouse family is well represented in Glen More and the four members exhibit very well how each species prefers a special kind of habitat. The largest member is the capercaillie, which lives in the real forests; a huge black turkey-like bird, the males are considerably bigger and darker than the reddish-brown females. They are shy and all one usually sees (or rather hears) is a huge bird crashing through the trees as it takes flight. They eat a variety of plants, such as the shoots of the bilberry bush, and later in the summer the fruits as well, but in the winter they eat pine shoots and it is then that one can recognise their distinctive droppings.

In the forest clearings and along the edge of the woods, black grouse occur in small numbers. The males are called black cocks and the females grey hens; in spring the black cocks gather on traditional display grounds called leks where they perform beautiful strutting displays accompanied by bubbling and wheezing sounds. As we move out on to the heather moors we enter the territories of red grouse; in Glen More these extend up to three thousand feet where they meet ptarmigan country. In winter, ptarmigan are pure white and merge in beautifully with the snowy surroundings; in spring they moult into a grey-brown vermiculated plumage but the wings remain white. These birds can often be seen around the ski-slopes on Cairngorm.

Wading birds include oystercatchers, lapwings, golden and ringed plovers, all of which nest in the area in small numbers. Oyster-catchers and lapwings are two of the earliest birds to return to Strathspey, in fact the first mild spell in late February or early March sees these two handsome black-and-white waders giving their distinctive calls as they return to their breeding grounds. Much later, during the month of May, we see the return from North Africa of one of Scotland's rarest waders—the dotterel, which breeds in small numbers on the high plateaux. They are tame birds not unlike a golden plover but with a more distinctive plumage; the females are more brightly coloured than the males and the parental roles are reversed with the cock bird incubating the three eggs and rearing the young.

Snipe, woodcock (usually seen "roding" or display-flighting over the woodlands at dusk—its distinctive calls being a grunt and a squeak) and curlew are summer visitors to the forest park, while common sandpipers, redshanks and greenshanks can be seen at Loch Morlich. The long-legged graceful greenshank, with its beautiful flutey call, is rarer now in Glen More than it used to be before the increase in re-afforestation, but the sandpipers, forever bobbing up and down on stones at the water's edge, are well distributed round the loch shore. Black-headed gulls are frequent scavengers around camp sites and car parks, and even go up on to the high tops, but they nest in colonies near the river Spey; other gulls such as common, herring and black-backs sometimes stop on the loch on their way by.

35

The first cuckoos start calling over the glen in the first days of May; the earliest date I have being 24 April. Tawny and long-eared owls breed in the woods. The latter is rarer but both are difficult to see although more often heard calling at night. Not so the short-eared owl which can sometimes be seen quartering the younger plantations during the day. Summer visitors like swifts, swallows, house and sand martins are often to be seen skimming over the surface of Loch Morlich after insects, sometimes they even hawk the high tops in fine weather later in the summer. A century ago the great spotted woodpecker had all but disappeared from the Highlands although a few may have remained in the big old forests of Glen More and Abernethy; now they are well distributed and can be heard drumming in the forest. They are handsome black-and-white birds with red patches under the tail, the male has a red patch on the back of the head and the juveniles a red crown.

Ravens are now very scarce visitors but crows are plentiful. Here in the Spey Valley we have a hybrid zone between the hooded and carrion crows so we might see grey and black hoodies, jet black carrion crows and hybrids of a mixture of greys and blacks. Rooks and jackdaws nest further down the glen.

Small birds in the forest are plentiful although after severe winters like 1961–62 and 1962–63 the numbers crash and birds like the tits and wrens are scarce for several years before they recover their numbers. The woods contain great, blue, coal and long-tailed tits but pride of place goes to the distinctive little crested tit. A small brownish bird with a distinctive black and white crest—its head-quarters in Britain have always been in the old Caledonian forests of Strathspey, although in recent decades it has extended its range in the Moray Firth region. The crested tit has a distinctive trilling call. It nests in holes usually excavated in dead pine trees; in winter it quite often comes to bird tables in rural gardens. It is the emblem of the Scottish Ornithologists Club. Treecreepers and wrens are well distributed through all the woods and another well known bird of the area is the dipper, shaped like a wren but much bigger, all black with a smart white breast. We usually see him bobbing on a stone in the middle of the river. They are early nesting birds, building their untidy nests in the river banks.

Redwings and fieldfares, mainly winter visitors from Scandinavia, pass through on migration and although both species have now started to breed in Scotland neither have nested in Glen More to our knowledge. Mistle thrushes, blackbirds and song thrushes are mainly summer visitors to the woods and a few ring ouzels nest on the craigs above the tree line. The white-rumped wheatears arrive in late March and April from Africa; they nest in holes in the ground on

36

open land and occur up to the mountain tops. A few pairs of stone-chats nest in Glen More although after the cold winters of the early sixties none returned to nest for ten years. They are never as common as in the Western Highlands but the whinchat is quite common in scrubland and young plantations. The brilliantly coloured red-tailed redstart is less common than it used to be but the willow warbler is as ubiquitous as ever. I must say its delightful song really livens up the birchwoods in the spring.

The tiny goldcrest is plentiful in the pine forests but the spotted flycatcher is less common and only spends the summer with us; they are mainly to be found in the areas of open mature trees. Occasion-ally pied flycatchers are seen and in some years one or two pairs breed in Speyside. The dunnock, or hedge sparrow, often nests in the junipers, some of which reach 15–20 feet; in spring we may hear the clear-carrying song of the tree pipit as it display flights in a forest clearing; while out on the moors is its commoner relative the meadow pipit. Pied wagtails arrive in March after spending the winter in England—they are so much part of the scene on highland roads in the summer catching insects on the bare tarmac. Small numbers of grey wagtails breed along the forest rivers; their name does not really do justice to their beautiful plumage with its brilliant yellow under-parts.

One of the commonest birds of the woods is the chaffinch; it is also a tame bird and will hop around our feet in search of crumbs. The male is a handsome bird with brick red under-parts, blue-grey head, brownish back and flashing black-and-white wings and tail; the female is much duller. They nest in all types of woods and their song is clear and distinctive. It is interesting that the highland chaffinches have their own dialect and you may notice that the ones in Glen More sing differently compared with the ones in England. In winter the chaffinches gather in flocks and live around the farms and crofts in the area; sometimes they are joined by the brambling. This migrant from Scandinavia has nested once long ago in Scotland and in the last week of June 1951 a male was heard singing at Loch Morlich but it did not find a mate.

Bullfinches are well distributed through the woods, especially the denser sections; in autumn and winter they range up on to the heather moors. Linnets and twites are local and scarce, but siskins and redpolls are sometimes common. The siskins are mainly found in the pine forests where they nest well out on high branches; the brightly-coloured male has a noisy twittering display flight which it performs above the tree tops. In late summer they gather together in quite large flocks, sometimes with redpolls, and may be seen feeding in the alder trees at the edge of lochs and rivers.

37

The pine woods of Speyside are well known for the local Scottish crossbill—a larger-billed crossbill which extracts and eats seeds from the cones of Scots pine and other conifers with a unique bill which is distinctly crossed at the end. The males are bright red, the females green and the youngsters streaky brown. Some summers they are joined by continental crossbills from Scandinavia which have come to this country on large scale migrations or "irruptions". To the practised ear the slightly smaller continental bird's callnote is "chip" compared to our own bird's "chup". House sparrows, yellowhammers and reed bunting occur in the valley, the latter in small numbers in boggy areas and around the loch shore. Another bunting lives on the mountains, the snow bunting, a black and white lark-like bird; in winter they gather in small flocks to feed on crumbs around the mountain car parks and chair-lifts, while in summer a few of them remain in Scotland to nest in distant corries where they feed their young on craneflies gathered around the melting snow fields. The smart black-and-white cock has rather a scratchy song delivered from the top of a rock, while his duller-plumaged mate incubates four or five eggs deep in a pile of scree—they are one of our rarest breeding birds.

From time to time, migrant birds pass through Glen More and over the Cairngorms and one might see surprising sightings in the area—for example on 13 June 1972 a fulmar petrel was seen flying through the pass of Ryvoan towards Loch Morlich, a seabird far from its normal haunts. Odd waders and wildfowl are occasionally identified on migration, while waxwings and great grey shrikes are nearly annual visitors to the Spey Valley. In six different summers a snowy owl has been seen on the high tops while a black tern hawked for insects over Loch Morlich on 18 August 1962, and lesser whitethroat and red-backed shrike have been observed at Glen More camp site in spring.

BEASTS

Red deer occur throughout the Highlands but nowadays there are many fewer in Glen More than there used to be in its deer forest days. Deer are not encouraged in the forest plantations so they are kept out by high deer fences; they are also shy and so most of them shun areas heavily used by people. Some are still to be found on Cairngorm and some still move down into the forest for shelter and grazing. The male of the red deer is a stag, the female a hind and the young is called a calf. Stags are most impressive in the mating or rutting season in October; then they are in fine condition, sometimes very dark after rolling in their mud wallows, and it is a wonderful experience to hear the stags roaring in the glens and corries on a clear frosty autumn evening. The stag's antlers are shed each spring and the new horns take about three months to grow; to start with they are covered with soft skin called velvet. The calves are born in early July and the hind chooses a quiet area of long, sheltered heather to have her young. For some time the young calf will lie down and hide in the long heather at the approach of danger but soon it scampers after its mother all the time.

In the woods we are more likely to meet roe deer; they are much smaller than red deer and live in small family groups, rather than herds, in the pine and birch woods. The male is called a buck, the female a doe and the young a kid. The young are born in late May and June, usually one but sometimes twins. The bucks hold territories in the woods and one can often see young trees which have been frayed and stripped by the deer marking their territories. Roe have a bark not unlike a dog. Roe deer are more easily seen in early morning and evening when they move out of the thicker parts of the forest to graze in the clearings and forest edges; sometimes they move out on farm fields. Forest rides and the edge of the loch are a good place to spot them.

Red squirrels are well distributed throughout Speyside; it is hard to believe that they were nearly extinct in the early nineteenth century when their numbers had dramatically declined—the result it is thought of the huge destruction of the natural pine forests and severe winters. Some survived in Rothiemurchus and now, despite persecution as forest pests earlier this century, they are common and are unmolested except by cars when crossing the forest roads!

The squirrels of this area have red tails which become very pale and faded. Some of them become very tame especially at lay-bys and bird-tables; occasionally they are a nuisance when they empty rubbish bins in search of scraps and scatter litter on the roadside— maybe the bins should be squirrel-proof. Their main food is the seed of Scots pine and we may see them sitting in the trees chewing up a pine cone and eating the seeds; the chewed up cones fall to the ground and are a good way of telling whether squirrels are present. They will also eat other seeds and nuts, and will sometimes eat eggs and young birds of tree nesting species, like siskin and crossbill. The squirrels build their dreys out of twigs, leaves and grass up in the trees and these can look like birds nests—here the young squirrels are born.

Foxes, wildcats and badgers all occur in the forest but all are very difficult to observe; we may see badger setts on our walks, or smell the musty presence of a fox, or see one crossing the road in our car headlights; but it is only when the snow is on the ground that their tracks really show their presence. The red fox hunts all over Glen

39

More and the surrounding moors, at times they even visit the mountains. Early morning is the best time to catch a glimpse of a fox returning from a night's hunting or catching a few mice before laying up for the day. One morning very early in the Sluggan, a fox passed me by a few yards as it searched piles of old brushwood for mice—it was so intent on its task that it passed me as I sat on a rock. The local foxes eat a great variety of food, including carrion, small mammals, ground-nesting birds as well as berries and insects; sometimes they tackle lambs and domestic poultry and for this they are hunted.

Foxes live in dens, sometimes these holes are in sandy banks in the forest or they may be isolated rocky screes on the hills. One of the dens is used for breeding purposes and here the young are born, and on spring days one may with luck see them playing outside the burrow. These dens can be easily identified by the litter of feathers, bones and fur lying about the entrance and the ground will be flattened by the youngsters' antics.

Badgers also live underground but their burrows are in groups or setts, usually they are on a sandy bank in a wood or plantation, either pine forests or birch woods. Large mounds of sand are piled outside the holes and are an indication of the excavations underground. Badgers get most of their food in the woodlands after dark; there they eat a great variety of food, such as bulbs, shoots, berries, worms, beetles, small animals, eggs and young birds. The best time to see these animals is to sit quietly at dusk downwind from the sett and with luck one might see the black and white striped face of the badger emerge from the hole as long as one is quiet and can put up with the midges!

Wildcats are even more difficult to observe despite the fact that they are well distributed over the area. Very rarely one may be disturbed in the forest but the more usual view is of a large bushy tailed tabby crossing the road in the winter, illuminated by the car headlights. They were very scarce at the beginning of the century, but since the 1950s they have increased and recolonized deserted areas; the increase in dense plantations has been to their advantage. The main food is rabbit and small animals and birds; the wildcat's home is a hole among rocks or under a tree.

Otters are present throughout the length of the river Spey and they move up the smaller rivers and burns, and visit lochs like Loch Morlich. Fortunately the number of areas where otters gain sanctuary is increasing and it is to be hoped that their numbers will increase again. It is a wonderful sight to watch a family of otters playing in the reeds and floating-logs at the water's edge on a fine summer's evening; the spectacle is enhanced by their keeping in

Plate 15. Dinghy sailing on Loch Morlich.

Plate 16. Purple Saxifrage.

Plate 17. Dwarf Cornel.

Plate 18. Six-metre Mackereth Corer takes off from the bed of Loch Morlich with 6,000 years of history in its sample tube.

Plate 19. Crossbills feeding young.

Plate 20.   Dotterel.

Plate 21. Wild Cat.

Plate 22.   Reindeer born at Glenmore below Cairngorm. The males have much larger antlers than the cow and her calf.

Plate 23.   Reindeer bull in rut on Airgiod Meall. This bull has been marked with red to distinguish it from a stag in the stalking season.

Plate 24. Mr. Utsi supervising his reindeer herd on the Cairngorms.

Plate 25. Feeding a reindeer calf.

contact with their musical whistles. They feed on a variety of fish, including small trout and eels, as well as frogs at spawning time. Pine martens became extinct in Strathspey in the last century and despite recent extensions in their range from the West Highlands, they have not yet returned to live in Strathspey. Let's hope they do.

Stoats and weasels both occur in the valley; the latter being rather scarce. Stoats are interesting because up here they change their coats in early winter and become a dazzling white with a black tip to the tail—then the stoat is called an ermine. This change in colour is of great advantage to the stoat when the snow is on the ground, but in mild winters with little or no snow he looks rather out of place. Stoats range throughout the forests and fields, but more commonly in farming areas although they do visit the mountain tops. The principal prey is rabbit and they quite often kill and drag away rabbits larger than themselves. If you are driving along a road and you see a stoat run away from a dead rabbit, you will find that, if you stop your car twenty or so yards from the rabbit and turn off the engine, the stoat will return for its prey and you will get a good view of this bold little hunter.

The mountain hare also changes into a white coat. In winter, they start turning white in October and most of them are really white hares in December, January and February. The full dark coat is complete by May; then they are brown with a bluish cast, giving them their name "blue hare", they are smaller than common hares, have noticeably shorter ears and brown eyes. They are rather scarce on Cairngorm and its foothills, but on some nearby moors they occur in very large numbers; in winter they come down into the forest edges and cultivated lands.

Moles and hedgehogs are common; the former is abundant and mole hills are a frequent sight on fields throughout Strathspey. Some occur in the most isolated crofts and pastures. Hedgehogs tend to be lower down in the deciduous woods and in farmlands. Small mammals include common and pygmy shrews, bank and field voles and wood mice—all are well distributed and reasonably common. Water voles occur in two colour varieties, brown and black, the latter is predominant in our area and in their jet black coats and snub noses they are charming little rodents. Usually all we see is a splash as they dive into the water from the bank; surprisingly they also occur high in the hills.

Bats are not as common as further south, both in numbers or varieties, but we have identified at least three species living in the valley. It is easy to see small bats flitting about forest clearings or around large houses at dusk, but quite a different matter to identify them. This can be more easily achieved if one finds a daytime

41

roost; pipistrelle, long-eared and Daubenton's bats have been identified in Strathspey. The last-named is usually associated with rivers and lochs.

FISH, AMPHIBIANS AND REPTILES

The Spey is a famous river for salmon and some of them reach the higher burns of the forest to spawn; most of the lochs contain trout and pike are also well distributed. A few lochs, such as Einich and Insh, contain char. Eels move up most of the rivers and there are several species of small fish. Frogs are still plentiful in the Highlands, and it is surprising where they are seen, some of them spawning in pools and bogs as high as 3,000 feet. Toads are less common but widespread on the lower ground, while newts occur in some lochans. Lizards are fairly common in a variety of habitats, including the open pine forests; slow worms are scarcer and adders are near enough absent from the Glen. There are many interesting butterflies, moths and other insect groups both in the forest and on the exposed mountains; the most obvious being the wood ant with its large ant hills, a distinctive feature of the pine forest.

WILD LIFE CONSERVATION

In past centuries, the fauna of Glen More as elsewhere in Scotland was influenced by man as he changed the environment by extensive felling and exploitation of the Caledonian forests and by burning, aggravated by intensive persecution of birds of prey by keepers and the collecting of adults and eggs of rare birds by collectors. Many of these changes have been well documented. More recent habitat changes involving changes of land use and re-afforestation have caused a decrease in Glen More in the numbers of greenshanks and lapwings who prefer burnt and close-cropped areas.

But the recent history of change in Glen More is principally concerned with tourism; in the 1950s Glen More and the Cairngorms were still remote, travel was still difficult and only a few people reached the forests and high tops. Fifteen years ago the road from Coylumbridge was improved and a new road was built up the mountain to Coire Cas; all the great changes on the ski slopes and at Aviemore have occurred in the last decade and the numbers of visitors all year round have increased by leaps and bounds. It is wonderful that so many people can come and enjoy the beauty, peace and fresh air of the area. Many gain enjoyment and relaxation in watching the wild life. What a crime it would be if we allowed our activities to permanently damage the flora and fauna of this wonderful area—if we destroyed the very things that we came to see. New tourist developments arrive in Strathspey with amazing speed but, alas, no such urgency is applied to the need for a new approach to the protection and management of the superb area of mountain wilderness stretching from Strathspey to Deeside and westwards to Drumochter. A loss of wilderness and wild life is already evident and an indication of future trends unless a strong and positive overall approach to conserve the area is taken before long.

Many birds and animals are not noticeably affected by people but others like eagles and red deer are shy and will not tolerate undue disturbance. At least one Cairngorm eagle eyrie appears to have been deserted after nearly a decade of failure due to unwitting disturbance, alas the most critical period in an eagle's breeding cycle is around the busy Easter period when they have new laid eggs. The weather is often cold and if the birds are kept off the nest for any length of time the eggs are chilled.

The rare peregrine falcon on its cliff eyrie has also suffered some disturbance, but they are more tolerant than eagles and are still breeding successfully. Close at hand the numbers of breeding waders and ducks on Loch Morlich have decreased, this being most true of oystercatchers and ringed plovers which used to nest on the sandy beach. On the mountains we now see crows and black-headed gulls in search of scraps left by visitors—in the past it was not worthwhile for these avian scavengers to visit the barren mountain tops. Now they are there how will they affect the small populations of rare birds like dotterel and snow buntings?

Scotland's birds are also being influenced by a changing climate; colder, later springs and a more continental climate in the last decade have apparently been the reason why Scandinavian species have started to colonise or re-appear in the Highlands. The ospreys have returned, the snowy owl has bred in Shetland, the numbers of dotterel and snow buntings are high, and northern birds like redwing, fieldfare, wood sandpiper and bluethroat have nested in the Spey Valley. On the debit side, some birds like the corncrake and nightjar have gone, and other species like the redstart have become scarce in recent years, the latter possibly a result of climatic changes in the birds' winter quarters in the southern Sahara. It is a most exciting time for the ornithologist as new species attempt to breed in the country, but will the trend continue or will the weather become warmer and the northern birds retreat?

We can do nothing about changes due to the climate but we can, and must, try to prevent serious damage to the wild life of this unique area from increased human pressures or pollution. Special protection of individual pairs of very rare birds can be undertaken as at Loch Garten with the ospreys, and a system of sanctuary, or quiet, areas could be established where birds and animals, at certain periods of the year, may be left in peace.

The individual can also do his bit towards the conservation of the birds and animals of Glen More:

Please do not disturb nesting birds or parent birds with young; watch them from a safe distance with binoculars.

Please do not visit the nests of rare birds; and remember it is illegal to visit or photograph the occupied nests of very rare birds like eagles and falcon.

Please do not touch young deer or other young animals if you find them lying hidden in the grass.

BOOKS TO READ

There are quite a few books about the Cairngorms, but some of the older ones about wild life are difficult to obtain. Three birds, greenshank, snow bunting and dotterel, have been the subjects of important monographs by Desmond Nethersole-Thompson, much of the research being carried out in this area, two were published by Collins and the *Snow Bunting* by Oliver & Boyd. Two recent books on the birds and animals of the area include a Royal Society for the Protection of Birds publication: *Ospreys and Speyside Wild Life* by George Waterston and Roy Dennis, published in 1973, while an impressive and very interesting book called *The Cairngorms— their Natural History and Scenery* by Desmond Nethersole-Thompson and Adam Watson was published by Collins in 1974—it is a *must* for anyone really interested in this wonderful region and its wild life.

Roebuck

THE HERD OF REINDEER

By Dr. Ethel John Lindgren

FIELD-GLASSES are trained on the high corner and the fringes of Glen More Forest in the hope of catching a glimpse of Britain's only herd of reindeer (*Rangifer tarandus*). Enigmatic, neither wild nor tame, the "bulls", "cows", "calves" and gelded "oxen" are much discussed by scientists, veterinary surgeons, naturalists, broadcasters, tourists and the Press.

Antlers and bones of reindeer have been found in prehistoric caves and on sites excavated even in southern England, but the last reindeer known to have survived the mediaeval chase were hunted by Vikings in Caithness, according to the Orkneyinga Saga, about 800 years ago. A few which were imported as curiosities in the 18th and 19th centuries, apparently without herders, soon disappeared.

In 1947 Mr. Mikel Utsi saw the Cairngorms through a late April snowstorm and diagnosed "reindeer country". Lichens, over-looked by many experts because they are often hidden beneath short heather, proved so abundant that he resolved to bring selected animals from his own Swedish Lapland herd to Scotland. Official obstacles were surmounted through the representations of the Reindeer Council of the United Kingdom founded in 1949, and the Scottish Council (Development and Industry). Small consignments arrived, 1952-1955, from Norrbotten via Narvik, travelling over a thousand miles by lorry, train, boat and horse-box. In 1961 a bull and some cows were brought from southern Norway to forestall inbreeding. On these five journeys no animal was lost or injured.

Nevertheless close confinement, which continued during four weeks' quarantine in the urban air of Edinburgh, Glasgow, or Newcastle-on-Tyne, told heavily on the wide-ranging reindeer. Regulations imposed for the experiment restricted the first arrivals to fenced ground for nearly two years, and in the hot, wet summer of 1953 there were casualties from fly-strike. However, observation of the reindeer dispersed official and private fears. In 1972 the vigorous young bull "Kivi", born to a Russian reindeer cow in Whipsnade Park, was added to the Cairngorm herd and fathered at least seven of the 1973 calves.

Early in 1954 the Forestry Commission allowed the herd to use the splendid expanse of lichen-covered slopes south and east of Loch Morlich up to the sky-line where they still roam. The big forest fire of 1960 unfortunately depleted both the fenced grazing below Moormore, generously leased in 1952 by Lt.-Col. J. P. Grant, M.B.E., of Rothiemurchus, and the lichen cover on a small fenced

45

plantation in Queen's Forest which had been chosen in 1953 to demonstrate that conifers are not harmed by reindeer. The higher pasture up to the summits has been administered by the Highlands and Islands Development Board from 1972.

The Department of Agriculture in Edinburgh recognised in 1956 that reindeer could live and breed in Scotland. As no special restrictions remained, the Reindeer Company Ltd. was free to try to build up a herd well adapted to local conditions. By the summer of 1971 it consisted of 91 head, many reindeer representing the second or third generation in Scotland. The natural increase has been partly offset almost every year by one or two accidents, by the elimination of animals not required for breeding, by slaughter for meat and by live sales to parks in England and Scotland. Reindeer occasionally vanish without trace. Yet the slow, steady rise in numbers of the native herd was not interrupted until 1964, when dogs worried the cows before the calving season. Dogs off the lead are a serious menace to the herd. The rise in numbers continued, however, until 1971 and 280 reindeer in all have been born at Glen More, 1963-1973. The herd is now stabilised at 70-80 head.

Research is a major objective and extensive records have been kept. A new spraying technique has minimised the insect problem. The de-horning of a few male calves and stilboestrol implants on some mature animals were undertaken experimentally to add weight, which in a Scottish-born reindeer bull reached 295 lb. One cow calved successfully several times after a caesarian operation, probably the first ever attempted on a reindeer, and another caesarian, in which the mother again survived, produced a calf which lived for 18 hours. The birth of calves to mothers artificially inseminated with fresh and with frozen semen, in 1972 and 1973, is a remarkable achievement (see Dott & Utsi, 1973).

Since Mr. Nicholas Labba's return to Norrbotten, Sweden, in 1954, herding has been carried out by Highlanders or Englishmen, closely supervised by Mr. Utsi when he is on the Reserve. The Reindeer Council's desire to spread knowledge of reindeer farming is best fulfilled when visitors accompany Mr. Utsi or the Keeper to inspect the animals. Thousands do so annually and often boys or a whole family find themselves helping to corral the reindeer or shift them to new pasture. Sometimes an ox carries equipment or provisions on a pack-saddle; in winter there may be time for sleighing. Arrangements can usually be made at Reindeer House, a stone-faced lodge east of the Glen More camp site, or by letter to the Company's administrative office, Newton Hill, Harston, Cambridge CB2 5NZ. Reindeer bulls should not, of course, be approached closely in October, during the rut, but the fiercest bulls are fenced in at that time.

The lichen *Cladonia rangiferina* is well-known as "reindeer moss", but *Cl. alpestris, Cl. sylvatica*, other ground lichens and several rock and tree lichens are important elements in reindeer fodder in Lapland and the Cairngorms. Red deer have not been reliably reported to eat lichens unless they are starving and there is little overlap in diet, although reindeer enjoy the first green grass of spring.

Reindeer meat, fresh or smoked, is a popular food not only in arctic and subarctic regions but throughout Scandinavia, in Germany and in the United States, always fetching a good price. In 1951-1952, 400 tons imported from Sweden by London firms were quickly bought by the general public. Reindeer hide tans to a suede-like finish for luxury gloves and hand-bags. Skins with the hair on, simply stretched and dried, make the warmest of ground sheets for explorers. Reindeer milk is delicious and as rich as cream. To acquire a pair of antlers is often a tourist's dream, but most of those in Scotland are still kept for exhibition and study.

BIBLIOGRAPHY

DOTT, H. M. and UTSI, M. N. P.
1973: Artificial Insemination of Reindeer (*Rangifer tarandus*). *Journal of Zoology.* Vol. 170, pp. 505–508

DOTT, H. M. and UTSI, M. N. P.
1971: The Collection and Examination of Semen of the Reindeer (*Rangifer tarandus*). *Journal of Zoology,* Vol. 164, pp. 419–424

ASCHAFFENBURG, R., GREGORY, MARGT E., Kon, S. K., ROWLAND, S. J., and THOMPSON, S. V.
1962: The Composition of the Milk of the Reindeer. *Journal of Dairy Research,* Vol. 29, pp. 324–328

STEPHEN, DAVID
1963: (16 May) Controlling Scotland's Wild Deer. *Country Life,* pp. 1102–1103

UTSI, M. N. P.
1957: The Future of Reindeer in Scotland. *Oryx,* Vol. 4, pp. 39–42

KETTLE, D. S. and UTSI, M. N. P.
1955: *Hypoderma diana* (Diptera, Oestridae) and *Lipoptena* (Diptera, Hyppoboscidae) as Parasites of Reindeer (*Rangifer tarandus*) in Scotland, with notes on the Second-stage Larva of *Hypoderma diana. Parasitology,* Vol. 45, pp. 116–120

RITCHIE, JAMES
1920: The Influence of Man on Animal Life in Scotland. C.U.P.

WATSON, GEOFFREY
1964: Reindeer in Scotland. *Wild Life Observer,* No. 8, p. 13.

1956: Reindeer in the Scottish Highlands. *Veterinary Record,* Vol. 68, p. 278

TEGNER, HENRY
1963: (19 December) The Sleigh Team of St. Nicholas. *Lady*

47

A path through the Pinewoods

When in the years of war the lumbermen have come to our forest
And tossed aloft the pigeon's wing and unhoused the squirrel,
And driven raw wounds into the golden-brown pines,
And dragged the fallen and humiliated timber at the rear of the arbitrary tractor
They have wrought no abiding hurt;
Heather and grass conceal
The axe-made weal,
And in the summer the dragonfly drives his flame across the sawdust embers,
And not a hollow remembers
The commanding rasp of saw, the thunder of ponderous wheel.

— William Jeffrey

FORESTS AND PLANTATIONS

BY JAMES FRASER AND ROBERT A. INNES

GLEN MORE FOREST is part of an old natural pine forest, which originally extended along the whole Spey valley into its side valleys and corries up to an elevation of about 1,500 feet above sea-level. By the end of the seventeenth century, the original area of the forest had been much reduced by grazing, by agricultural cultivation, by accidental and wilfully kindled fires, and by a relatively small amount of ordinary forest exploitation work. Other well-known parts of this big forest are Rothiemurchus, Abernethy,

Dulnain and Glen Feshie. The small amount of agricultural development in the valley restricted the local demands for timber, and roads
were almost non-existent in these forest areas. The survival of a very
substantial part of the natural forests to the beginning of the
eighteenth century was due to their inaccessibility. But water
transport of logs and sawn timber, on the side streams and in the
main valley, began at an early date, and probably became important about the end of the fifteenth century, when building of fishing
boats and small ships was encouraged by the State. Although pine
was the principal tree in the Glen More forest, other trees were
birch and alder. The writer of the *First Statistical Account* of the
parish (in 1794) draws attention to the handicap imposed on
agriculture by the lack of a good local supply of hardwoods.

The earliest recorded use of the Glen More Forest is as a hunting
ground, first for the Stewarts of Kincardine, then for the Kings of
Scotland, and later for the Dukes of Gordon. The earliest Scottish
forest laws were directed by the sporting interests of the forests. At
the best, these laws were fairly negative in character, and they
probably received as little attention in Glen More as did the later
more positive laws directing the planting and regeneration of woods.
"Glenmore" in his *Highland Legends*, published in 1789, refers to a
special privilege of collecting "torch" wood in Glen More Forest
given to the Duke of Gordon's tenants from areas outside Glen More,
and this custom was probably much older. The few small agricultural
tenants in the clear spaces doubtless enjoyed certain limited rights of
pasturing in the forest, and they made full use of them. They also
made use of birch bark and alder bark for tanning, and birch bark
for roof cover, and they must have supplied their small local needs
for timber and firewood from the forest. The peeling of bark from
living trees was apparently a common forest offence in Scotland,
and it remains common in some northern countries.

The value of timber in the Spey valley, even when reckoned with
reference to the low prices of the times, remained small until road
and water communications had been improved. The *First Statistical
Account* states that in the period about 1677 to 1700, a man might
still enjoy the right of harvesting the timber which he could cut with
an axe and saw, for the payment of an annual rent of 5s. and a pound
of tobacco. The forest accounts of Rothiemurchus Estate, which is
close to Glen More, for the year 1766, show that the prices of trees
had risen to three merks each (3s. 4½d.) and that the Estate had a
fair local trade in trees—logs, deals, backs, flaichs (rough gates or
hurdles) and oars. By 1766, several large contracts with timber
merchants had been arranged by local landowners. Sir Thomas
Dick Lauder, in his notes added to the third edition of Gilpin's

Forest Scenery (1834), records that, on the Rothiemurchus Estate, the profits during the period of intensive timber working often amounted to £20,000 per year. The figure need not be taken as very exact, but it certainly shows a marked rise in timber values.

The early use of the timber from the Spey valley for local boat building has been mentioned already, and that use continued right down to the middle of the nineteenth century. Although hopes of selling the timber from the district for Admiralty use were raised from time to time, no very big trade appears to have developed. A list of the boats built at the mouth of the Spey is given in the *Statistical Account* of 1794. During the late eighteenth century the manufacture of wooden water pipes was developed. The pine trunks were bored at Rothiemurchus, and shipped to London for use in the New River and similar public water supply schemes.

Big-scale timber operations in the Spey area began about 1622. Nairne refers to one sale by Sir John Grant at that date. The cash involved was £20,000 Scots (£1,666 sterling). A much-recorded transaction is that of the York Timber made in 1728 with Rothiemurchus Estate. The amount of the contract there was £7,000 sterling. The transaction is described by the parish minister of the time as a "stock jobbing business", and the Company as "the most profuse and profligate set that were ever heard of in this corner". The Glen More owner of the time appears to have been interested in the prospects of a profitable deal with the York Timber Company, but without result. Nairne states that several attempts at a sale were made by the Glen More estate before it closed a bargain, in 1784, with Messrs. Osbourne and Dodsworth of Kingston-upon-Hull. The York Timber Company did not complete their payments or their contract with Rothiemurchus, and operations were brought to a close by suitable legal action by the Rothiemurchus proprietor. In spite of the bad reputation of the York Company men, it has been freely admitted that they taught the local men a great deal about big-scale operations, including the construction of big rafts for floating down the Spey. One Aaron Hill has received special mention as the man responsible for the improvement of the Spey rafts.

A few interesting details of the Glen More 1784 contract have been obtained through the kindness of Sheriff Grant of Rothiemurchus. The facts are recorded in a document dated 1808. The felling in Glen More by Osbourne and Dodsworth was restricted to an area of about one fifth of the total timber area. Trees below a certain breast height measurement were excluded from the contract. The working period of the contract was 26 years. The Company worked in perfect harmony with the estate, and the owner of the estate constructed one road for the Company. The Company profited from the experience of the York Company by making greater concentration of the saw-mill work. Towards the end of the contract period, when it became unprofitable for the Company to maintain their big working squads and staff, on account of the scattered nature of the work, an arrangement was made by which the Company gave up its right to any further timber cutting, and they received a repayment of £500. Sir Thomas Dick Lauder, in his work of 1834, records that "The Glen More forest is fast replenishing itself" (by natural regeneration). This record should be read along with the statement (about replanting) of the Ordnance Gazetteer, and along with statements that the area was used as a sheep farm, after the first big felling. It does not appear that any serious reconstruction of the forest was done by planting before the Forestry Commission began its work in 1924.

There are two further exploitation periods to be recorded in Glen More. In the war period 1914-1918, the Canadian Forestry Corps removed a very great part of the natural crop; and again in 1945-1947, war fellings extended over an area of about 200 acres and removed a volume of about 400,000 cubic feet.

Accounts have been given of the timber floating operations in the Spey valley by "Glenmore", by the writer of the *First Statistical Account*, by Nairne and by "A Highland Lady"—Mrs. Smith of Baltiboys (*née* Grant). The last named account is a very attractive piece of descriptive writing. Two distinct stages of the operations should be distinguished, loose log floating on the side streams and raft floating on the Spey. The floating on the side valleys was controlled by dams and sluices. The felled logs were drawn by horses to the side of the burns and there were peeled and allowed to dry out. When the dams were full and other weather conditions favourable, the logs were pushed into the side burns and conveyed either to the Spey or to saw-mill sites in favourable positions for working and further transport operations. In Glen More, there were two lines of export of this first type—down the Druie and down the Sluggan.

The remains of the last known floating dam, at Loch Einich, are illustrated in Plate 6.

In the Spey before the days of the big type of raft introduced by the York Timber Company, the rafts were very simple. When logs were transported, about eight logs were roped together with horse hair ropes. The raft was guided by a man sitting in a *curach*, which was simply a small coracle, and in addition the logs were controlled from the banks by ropes. The *curach* was carried back from the mouth of the Spey or from the saw-mill site by one man. When deals formed the raft, ten to twelve dozen were probably secured by osiers or birch twigs passed through holes in the ends. Those

51

may be the holes referred to by Edmund Burt, an eighteenth-century writer on the customs of northern Scotland, when describing the partition and ceiling boards of Inverness houses. When the big form of raft was developed, the foundation of the raft was made of heavy logs in the form of a brander or grid and those logs were bolted together. Above this framework, other logs or spars or sawn timber were piled and secured. The raft was guided by two men using sweeps or big oars which were left at the point where the raft was broken up. The men of Knockando were the expert tradesmen for the Spey rafting. In the early history of rafting on the Spey, the period was restricted only by the suitable spate periods. By 1808 it is recorded in a Rothiemurchus record that rafting between the dates 15th May and 25th August was prohibited. Fishing interests of the Duke of Gordon were responsible for that restriction.

Written records and other evidence show the progress of the method of working the forest products of the area. The 1794 *Statistical Account* refers to planks prepared by splitting logs with axes and wedges, and by subsequent dressing with adzes and axes. The development of the bigger and more elaborate water-mills was due probably to the big "invading" companies, although small water-mills had been used earlier by local merchants. By 1800 a form of water-worked frame saw had been developed. Later, steam- and diesel-powered mills replaced the water-driven types.

Forsyth, in the account which he has written about Glen More, records that it was converted into a sheep run in the period 1831 to 1841, and that in 1859 the forest was cleared of sheep and was turned into a deer forest. If one remembers and accepts the statement by Sir Thomas Dick Lauder, quoted above, it can be fairly safely assumed that by 1831 natural regeneration had restocked the greater part of the forest following the destruction of the first big fellings. The intensive use of land by sheep can be as destructive to the soil fertility as heather burning, but in Glen More it is not probable that it was ever possible to maintain a heavy stock of sheep. (At all events, the period of intensive sheep use must have been short.) This is due to the severe winter climatic conditions. For similar reasons, the Glen More area could not at any time have maintained a very heavy deer stock. Rabbits are not plentiful in the forest, and they are also unable to reach real destructive numbers on account of the severe winters. Although the destructive powers of sheep are fully appreciated, it is difficult in the case of Glen More to accept the sheep as the full real cause of the failure of natural regeneration from 1834 to the present day.

In 1923 the Glen More property was acquired by the Forestry Commission, which started its operations there in 1924. It was realised at the outset that the profitable growth of timber would only be possible on the lower slopes of the hills. An elevation of 450 metres (about 1,500 feet), which is roughly the upper limit in Speyside of good Caledonian pine forest, was accepted as the highest contour to which planting for timber production could be undertaken. This meant that some 1,500 hectares (some 3,500 acres) or approximately a quarter of the estate was regarded as plantable. The balance of 3,550 hectares (or 9,000 acres) consisting of mountain land was excluded by deer fencing from the plantable ground, and was later made freely available to the public when the whole area was created a Forest Park in 1948. (1 hectare = 2.47 acres).

When the estate was acquired in 1924, there still remained, despite the long history of exploitation, 80 hectares of native Caledonian pines, not in one single block of woodland, but dispersed throughout Glenmore in dense groups of small extent, or as extensive areas of open woodland of individual trees.

These remnants, mostly over 150 years old, have been preserved and although relatively small in area still figure prominently in the forest landscape at Glenmore, particularly around the shores of Loch Morlich, in the Ryvoan Pass and on the lower slopes of the Cairngorms.

It was accepted in 1924 that natural regeneration of the native pinewoods in Glenmore would not achieve the restocking of the degraded forest soils with any degree of certainty. The Forestry Commission therefore decided that its main objective of producing marketable timber would best be achieved by planting. However an area of the native pinewood was selected, and enclosed by fencing, to find out whether any significant regeneration could be achieved in the absence of grazing animals. From 1930 a variety of experimental treatments to aid regeneration were tried, ranging from soil cultivation, disturbance of ground vegetation and direct seeding, but the results were disappointing.

In other parts of Glenmore, particularly on the sandy banks around Loch Morlich, where the ground vegetation is sparse, pines have regenerated vigorously in association with birch.

There have been two major phases of planting by the Forestry Commission. 540 hectares were planted between 1924 and 1935, followed by small annual programmes up to and during the war years. After the 1939-45 war there was another period of large scale planting from 1951 to 1965 when a further 540 hectares were planted. From 1966-1972 the balance of plantable ground, a relatively small area, was completed bringing the total area planted to date to 1,405 hectares.

Scots pine (658 hectares) covers half the area planted, followed by

Sitka spruce on about one-third of the area (407 hectares). Small areas of Norway spruce, lodgepole pine, Douglas fir, Japanese and European larches occupy the remainder of the area. The Scots pine was not raised from native stock but was grown from seed collected in the pine plantations of North-East Scotland.

The early planting was done by notching the young trees from a forest nursery directly into the undisturbed soil surface, but it soon became evident that improvement of the soil by drainage and cultivation was necessary for successful tree growth. Before the war, drainage and cultivation were done manually, but after the war, machines were designed to undertake this work, which led to significant improvements in tree growth, particularly with conifer species that are not native to Britain, such as Sitka spruce and lodgepole pine. More recently the application of mineral fertilisers, phosphate principally, to young trees has improved tree growth dramatically.

These developments are mirrored in the Glenmore woods where, in the older pre-war areas, south of Loch Morlich and Ryvoan mainly, growth is far from uniform, but in general Scots pine has succeeded better than other species. After the war, a large area north of the ski-road was mechanically cultivated preparatory to planting. Phosphate was applied to the trees shortly after planting and the resultant growth has been vigorous and uniform, in contrast to the rather uneven growth in the pre-war plantations.

Some of the older plantations have now reached the thinning stage. The current annual yield of thinnings is 1,000 cubic metres of timber and this will increase as more plantations reach the thinning stage. The harvesting of the timber provides continuous employment for forest workers and contractors. The principal market for thinnings is the Pulp and Paper Mill at Fort William. In order to get the timber out and to provide ready access to all parts of the forest in case of fire, a system of forest roads, extending to 35 kilometres has been constructed by the Commission's engineers. Although these roads are not open to cars, walkers are free to use them; but the Commission reserves the right to close them at times of extreme fire hazard.

RECREATION DEVELOPMENTS

The Forestry Commission's initial aim was to create forests to supply industry and people with wood, but more recently the recreational value of forests has come to be realised not only in Britain but in Europe and other countries throughout the world.

The Forestry Commission, recognising the special attractions of its estate in the Cairngorms declared it a forest park in 1948 with the title Glen More Forest Park.

A simple camp site was laid out in front of the old shooting lodge, which was also adapted for recreational use by leasing it, first to the Scottish Council for Physical Recreation and subsequently to the Scottish Youth Hostels Association who are the current tenants.

In the immediate post-war years when Glenmore was relatively remote and difficult of access, recreational use of the Park was limited to the more energetic visitors but in 1960 a single track road was constructed from Coylumbridge via Loch Morlich to the upper ski-slopes by the County Council. In the same year the Commission leased the ski development rights to the Cairngorm Winter Sports Development Board, a non-profit making body of mainly local interests who had the foresight to see the ski-ing potential of the mountains.

With the increasing popularity of the sport, the need for better access became obvious and in 1966/67 the road was reconstructed to a two-lane highway with easier gradients and terminal car parks. The ski-ing services, i.e. chairlift, ski-tows and restaurants have likewise been improved to meet the growing demand. (Present services are described elsewhere in this guide.)

Easier access coinciding with a general increase in the demand for leisure and recreational pursuits brought greater demands on the Forest Park. The Commission has met these by extending, modernising and innovating facilities, such as the redesigned caravan park, additional car park and picnic sites, the new Norwegian Hostel, toilets and information office. (Full details in the General Information section of this guide.) The Forestry Commission has also encouraged the public to enjoy the relative peace and isolation of the woodlands by setting out forest trails and treks, with descriptive booklets designed to guide and inform the public about the forest environment.

The Glen More woods differ from commercial plantations in their lack of uniformity caused by the varying age classes, species and growth rates. This diversity not only creates a forest of great amenity value to the visitor, but is an ideal habitat for a variety of birds and animals. The public's recreational needs bring great pressures on the forest environment and it will be the Commission's aim at Glen More to reconcile these with carefully planned timber production and conservation. Fire is one of the major hazards and the co-operation of the visitor is sought to reduce this danger to a minimum. ————————————

Note: In 1970, 2,422 hectares of the mountain land in the forest park, including the main ski-slopes were sold to the Highlands and

Islands Development Board, who have continued to lease the land to the former ski-ing organisation, which has been reconstituted and entitled the Cairngorm Sports Development Council. The land continues to be designated as lying within the Glen More Forest Park, permitting free public access on foot for recreational purposes.

LOCH MORLICH

on a spit of sand, a pine on tiptoe, enough
space under the roots for a man to walk through:
they're like a rusted grab abandoned by workmen
decades ago, somehow the tree's still alive

in a wide clearing, a floor of roots to walk over,
no growth, in the triangles of dry sand:
the ravel can never be unpicked, the loops all
uneven like a child's first attempt at weaving

in a fertile corner, with earth and junipers,
a giant pine on its side, almost as white as quartz:
it should be in a museum with metal rods
supporting its bones and learned estimates of its age

in the shallows, a stump (surely older still)
with two moulded roots sticking up like horns:
something has been retreating or advancing so
long and stubbornly only the gesture remains

—Robin Fulton

Plate 26.   A forest trail through ancient Caledonian pinewoods near the Allt Mor.

Plate 27. Power saw felling.

Plate 28. Debranching with the power saw.

Plate 29. Hauling out timber with a tractor and sulky.

Plate 30.   Winter climbers above the Coire an t'Sneachda.

Plate 31. Trekking party setting off for the Lairig Ghru.

Plate 32. Camping in Coire an Lochan.

Plate 33.   Clach Bharraig, Foundation Stone, near the old path leading up by the Windy Ridge to the Cairngorm summit.

Plate 34.   Bridge over Allt Mor on a forest trail.

Plate 35. An Lochan Uaine—the Green Lochan in the Ryvoan Pass.

Plate 36. The island stronghold of Loch an Eilein.

Plate 37. Loch Avon and the Shelter Stone Crag.

Cairn Lochan Corrie

SAFETY ON THE MOUNTAINS
By A. L. McClure, Q.P.M.,
Chief Constable of Inverness Constabulary

It is, perhaps, true to say that in no part of the world is there greater emphasis on sport and all forms of recreation than there is in this comparatively small country of ours. Indeed, our measure of success in this field of competition compares favourably with the best in the world. The determination to win, the desire to prosper, the zest for excitement and the love of pleasure, are all unmistakable characteristics of the British race. The spirit of adventure is self-evident, and, in fact, so manifest on occasions as to be inclined to displace prudence in the face of danger. This has not been more clearly illustrated than in the terms of cost to human life and limb in mountaineering accidents.

Mountaineering is undoubtedly one of the finest forms of recreation this country has to offer its youth: exhilarating, stimulating, challenging and—unfortunately what is not always appreciated—fraught with danger. Contrary to the somewhat hackneyed explanation, mountains are not climbed "because they are there"; rather, they are climbed because they have so much to offer. It is not always realised that in winter or summer these mountains demand the utmost respect if they are not to exact their grievous toll of life.

The number of accidents on our Scottish mountains within recent

57

years has been quite disturbing, particularly in the knowledge that most of them need not have happened had there not been such a flagrant disregard for the simple laws of safety. This needless waste of young lives is viewed with serious concern, to say nothing of the heavy strain on police manpower and other volunteer services in the discharge of both official and moral responsibilities to mankind. It is singularly regrettable that such a high percentage of those who fall victim to the perils of mountaineering are students from colleges and universities throughout the country; people of promise, a high standard of intelligence and education, whose potential contribution to society our country can ill afford to lose.

In Scotland, especially, in accordance with the constitutional laws of the country, mountain search and rescue organisation is officially the responsibility of the police. In the organisation the police are ably assisted by other interested bodies, such as local mountain rescue teams, Royal Air Force Mountain Rescue Teams, and Helicopter Support Group, the Army, the Ambulance Services, the British Red Cross Society, the Mountain Rescue Committee, and other interested bodies who give their services unstintingly in whatever capacity they are best suited.

Much is being done to educate the unwary in the etiquette of mountain safety, such as periodical "Police Call" programmes on both sound and television broadcasts, the exhibition of suitable posters and the dissemination of other advisory propaganda. Yet it continues to be an up-hill task to convince some people of the importance of being equal to the challenge before it is accepted. It is distressing to find that the sound advice so freely and seriously given should be all too often ignored, and with such tragic results.

As Chief Constable of this County in which there has been a most disturbing death-rate on the mountains during the last decade or so, I earnestly appeal to every young climber, and also to every young person who very soon may discover the magnetic power of the mountains, and for whom this article is intended, to treat the advice it contains as being a very personal message, and not at all to be dismissed lightly as being directed at someone else.

The rules of the game are but the basis of good, common sense, and are set out as follows:

GENERAL FITNESS
1. Mountaineering is an arduous and, sometimes, exacting sport, demanding physical fitness and mental alertness of no mean order. Do not think that you are fit for mountaineering if you have just vacated your office chair, or are just having a break from your

studies. Mountaineering is a real test of stamina, and you should leave it severely alone unless you are physically fit for it.

2. Learn as much as possible about mountaineering by reading books and asking questions of experienced climbers who will be delighted to tell you much more than the scope of this article permits. You will discover that there is much to learn.

CLOTHING AND FOOTWEAR
3. It is common knowledge that people have died on the mountains (a) because of inadequate clothing and (b) because of unsuitable footwear. You must provide for your protection against both weather and ground conditions.
4. Bear in mind that when the temperature is just on the freezing line at sea level there will be a minimum of 14 degs. of frost on the summit of Cairngorm, and perhaps as much as 22 degs. Make adequate provision for warm, windproof clothing, including gloves and headgear.
5. Suitable footwear is of the utmost importance. Either nailed or vibram-soled *boots* are recommended, preferably the former for all-round conditions, especially if you are to encounter ice or wet, slippery rocks. Your climbing boots should be a size larger than you wear in normal footwear, as this will enable you to wear two pairs of woollen stockings.

EQUIPMENT
6. As this article is intended for the guidance of the uninitiated it does not cover all the paraphernalia that is usually carried by the expert climber. To begin with you should limit your equipment to the bare necessities. An ice axe is essential if you encounter snow-slopes; but remember you must know how to use it. Its most important use is to prevent you crashing to destruction!
7. Any ideas of ambitious rope-work should be dispelled until you have had the benefit of expert instruction. You must carry a map, compass, whistle, torch and watch; but if you do not know how to use your map and compass you might as well leave them at home! It may sound incredible, but it is still true that many mountaineers have no idea how to use their map and compass. A slight error in navigation could lead you to destruction!

FOOD
8. Never attempt any form of mountaineering without a good supply of food. It is better to carry concentrated foods which do

not encumber you unduly. Glucose, chocolate and fruit are high on the list. The main thing is to ward off the pangs of hunger.

9. It is nothing but the height of folly to attempt any form of mountaineering alone. Go mountaineering alone and you are in gross breach of etiquette! There should never be less than three members in a mountaineering party so that, in the event of mishap, one member stays with the injured party while the third summons assistance.

10. Make sure that you have at least one experienced climber in the party, and do not make any stupid suggestions to him as to what should be done in the face of impossible conditions. Remember never to separate except in emergency.

PLANNING
11. You must plan carefully whatever it is you intend doing on the mountains. In winter time you must not forget to take into consideration the amount of daylight available. Route cards have been provided at police stations and other suitable places. These should be completed before setting out on an expedition and left with some suitable person. A sample is printed after the Hill Walks map. Having made your plan you must stick to it, or else abandon it and return home, but never abandon it in favour of something else without telling someone. There have been instances of climbers intimating their intention to climb in a certain area and, without further notice, changing their plan to something else. The inevitable consequences of such thoughtlessness in the event of mishap would be that searchers would be despatched to the area intimated, while you might be dying of exposure and injuries only a matter of half a mile away.

GLISSADING
12. From records of accidents occurring on the mountains it emerges that many have been due to careless glissading, such as glissading in misty conditions when snow slopes reach out over sheer cliff faces, and glissading in snow which is too soft, and in which it is impossible to break one's fall with an ice axe. Glissading calls for every possible care.

CONCLUSION
13. If all young climbers and, indeed, some of those who have already gained a measure of experience, and, perhaps, escaped mishap only by the Grace of God, pay attention to their more experi-

enced elders, refrain from tempting providence, and obey the simple, commonsense rules of the game, then we may look forward with confidence to an encouraging fall in the graph which has signified so much grief, entailed so much expenditure of physical effort, and incurred so much expense in the past.

The Shelter Stone

Once reached, a hilltop requires exploration:
once mapped, it tempts us both to stay
friended by wild birds, at home with heights
and weathers—how good to be exalted,
conspire with clouds and never go away!

— Tom Buchan

HILL WALKS
IN AND AROUND THE PARK

By B. H. Humble

Glen More and the surrounding Cairngorms provide many forest and hill walks of varying degrees of difficulty, length and scenic variety.

Several of these are described below, classified into forest and hill walks where there are clearly defined roads or tracks, and mountain routes and hill passes where there may be no clearly defined path and adequate preparations and equipment to face the risks and dangers of hill walking are essential.

The small scale map in the central inset is for general guidance only. All going on the hills should have either the Ordnance Survey's one inch to the mile "Tourist Map of the Cairngorms" or the newer one "High Tops of the Cairngorms" which is on the metric scale. All roads and paths mentioned in the text are shown on these maps.

FORESTS AND HILL WALKS

There are three waymarked forest trails of comparatively short length within easy distance of the central caravan site and information office suitable for families and young people. A small descriptive and interpretive booklet which guides the visitor along the trails can be purchased at the Information Office or the Camp Warden's Office.

Three longer hill walks within and beyond the Forest Park are now described.

RYVOAN AND RYNETTIN

The Pass of Ryvoan was the thieves' route of old—the escape route of cattle raiders from Speyside to the north, and the hill on the east side commemorates this—Creag nan Gall (the Hill of the Stranger). From the camp site the road goes past Glenmore Lodge and continues to Lochan Uaine (the Green Loch) in the heart of the pass. The water is of a translucent greenish blue and so clear that one can see the stones at the bottom. And of course it got that colour because the fairies used to wash their clothes in it and danced around the little conical hill just above it! Looking back from just beyond the lochan the view has attracted many an artist and photographer, with the lochan hemmed in by crags on either side, the forests beyond and the background of great mountains. The lochan has no visible outlet but drains below to the streams which run down to Loch Morlich.

Further on the road forks at the western boundary of the forest area, the track to the right leading over to Strath Nethy. Our route is to the left, up to Ryvoan Bothy, recently restored by the Mountain Bothies Association and a great haunt of hill walkers all the year round. It is well worth having a glimpse of the Visitors' Book which is kept within. Entering Rynettin Woods, a memorial stone is seen on a knoll to the left, erected "in remembrance of James Hamilton Maxwell, who loved these hills", a young man from Edinburgh who was killed at Ypres in the 1914–18 war. Passing Rynettin, a keeper's house, a charming road continues among woods alive with bird life past Forest Lodge to join a motorable road near Dell Lodge.

Returning by the same route the distance in all is about 14 miles.

THE SLUGGAN PASS

From the camp site walk along the Aviemore road. Near the west end of the loch a signposted road leads to the north with a parking place on the lochside nearby. Follow this road for about 3 miles to the Queen's Stone Memorial Cairn at the head of the pass. Here one realises the significance of the name "sluggan" (the gullet), as steep slopes fall away on either side to the river far below. Beyond this the old road continues north, but take the new one to the left which leads steeply uphill to the summit of Creag Ghreusaich (1,416 feet) and locally known as the TV hill. *Do not go near the pylon or building.*

This easily reached summit is a splendid viewpoint for the whole area with visibility in all directions—a great stretch of the Spey Valley from south-west to north-east, the lay-out of Cairngorm with its ski road and lifts, the cleft of the Lairig Ghru, the mass of Braeriach, the gap of Glen Einich and then Sgoran Dubh.

Returning by the same route to the lochside is about 6½ miles. An alternative return is to take the forest road marked Badaguish a mile before reaching the loch and just before reaching this hamlet branch right where a forest road leads back to the camp site. (Camp site to camp site about 8½ miles.)

GLEN EINICH

This glen can be approached either from Glenmore or Coylumbridge. From the former route, start at the Bailey bridge at the west end of Loch Morlich and continue as far as the cross roads in the forest, then downstream a little to the bridge erected by the Cairngorm Club about 5½ miles from the camp site. From the bridge the track leads west for about ¾ of a mile to join the road from Coylumbridge. This road, through Nature Reserve ground, has been much improved recently, and leads up the lovely glen, densely wooded in its lower part, then bare and open, culminating in Loch Einich which almost rivals Loch Avon in the grandeur of its surroundings, hemmed in by the crags of Sgoran Dubh on the west and Braeriach on the east. Formerly there were two bothies in the glen but these have long since disappeared. Loch Einich was used in the olden timber-floating days, when there were sluice gates at its mouth, but only a few stakes indicate these now (Plate 6). Again its water is being used to supply the increasing needs of the area and a pipe line has been laid up the glen. Once there was a shieling on the stretch of grass at the head of the loch where cattle came up for grazing. The loch itself is about 1¼ miles long and abounds in trout.

The return journey from the camp site is 23 miles, and from Coylumbridge 16 miles.

MOUNTAIN ROUTES

The following routes are introduced with a note of warning. Due to their height and open contour the mountains are subject to extreme weather conditions and weather precepts which hold in other mountainous areas are not always applicable here.

Map showing
HILL & MOUNTAIN WALKS

Forest   - - - -

Forest Roads   -------

Woodlands

Lochs

Heights up to 2000 feet

2000 to 2500 ft

2500 to 3000 ft

3000 to 3500 ft

3500 to 4000 ft

4000 feet and over

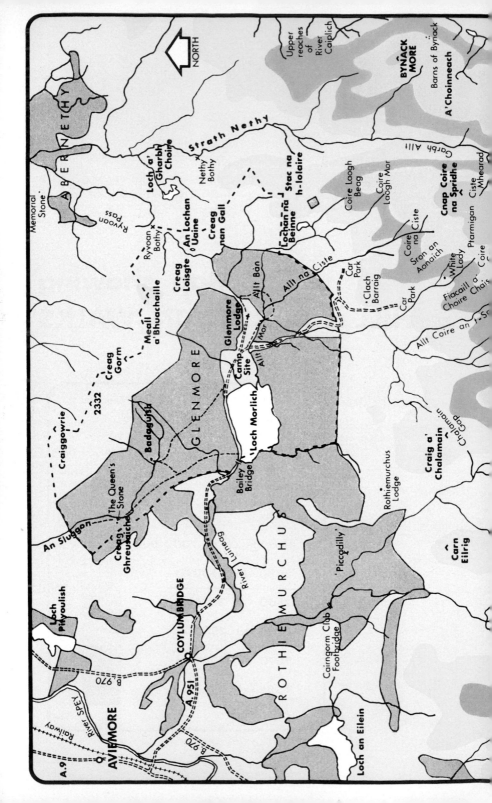

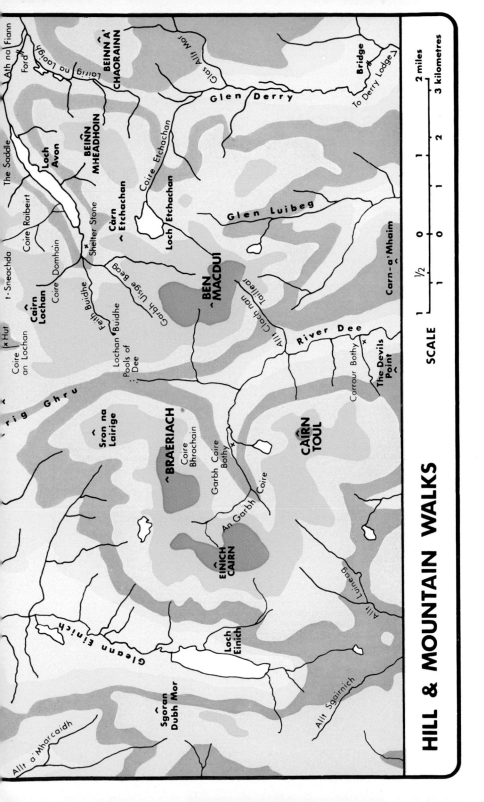

HILL & MOUNTAIN WALKS

SCALE

```
1      ½      0              1              2 miles
1      0              1              2              3 kilometres
```

Map labels:

Ath nal Fiann
Ford
The Saddle
Lairig na Laoigh
BEINN A' CHAORAINN
Glas Allt Mor
Bridge
To Derry Lodge
Glen Derry
BEINN MHEADHOIN
Coire Etchachan
Loch Avon
Coire Raibeirt
Coire Domhain
Shelter Stone
Càirn Etchachan
Loch Etchachan
Glen Luibeg
†-Sneachda
Coire an Lochan
x Hut
Cairn Lochan
Feith Buidhe
Garbh Uisge Beag
Lochan Buidhe
Pools of Dee
BEN MACDUI
Carn-a'Mhaim
Allt Clach nan Taillear
River Dee
rig Ghru
Sron na Lairige
BRAERIACH
Coire Bhrochain
Garbh Coire Bothy
An Garbh Coire
Corrour Bothy
The Devils Point
CAIRN TOUL
EINICH CAIRN
Gleann Einich
Loch Einich
Sgoran Dubh Mor
Allt a' Mharcaidh
Allt Luineag
Allt Sgairnich

Let us know
when you go
on our hills

Names and Addresses: Home Address and Local Address	Route
Time and date of departure;	Bad Weather Alternative:
Place of Departure and Registered Number of Vehicle (if any)	
Estimated time of Return:	Walking/Climbing (delete as necessary)

GO UP WELL EQUIPPED - TO COME BACK SAFELY

Please tick items carried:

Emergency Food	Torch	Ice Axe
Waterproof Clothing	Whistle	Crampons
(Colour -	Map	Polybag
Winter Clothing	Compass	First Aid
(Colour -		

Please complete and leave with Police, landlady, warden etc.
Inform landlady or warden to contact Police if you are overdue.

PLEASE REPORT YOUR SAFE RETURN.

Severe blizzards may and frequently do descend on the summits from September until the end of May, but steep snowslopes with crags and boulders below them may linger into summer to trap the unwary. Even in summer, however, the weather can deteriorate rapidly, enveloping the mountains in mist with a corresponding sharp drop in temperature. It is always advisable to obtain the local weather forecast in the morning which is displayed in the Information Centre above the camp site. This is much more detailed than the general forecast and indicates the likely conditions on the high plateaux that afternoon. Wind speeds on the mountains are often more than twice that at ground level.

Walkers should carry a compass, preferably of the Silva type, and be able to use map and compass properly. Suitable footwear, clothing and food reserves are essential.

In winter and spring the routes become mountaineering expeditions and only experienced climbers should attempt them.

MEALL A' BHUACHAILLE (2,654 feet)

This is a worthwhile first hill walk, and is best done from east to west. Take the road to Ryvoan Bothy, from where a marked path leads most of the way to the summit. Continue west down to the col between Bhuachaille and Creagan Gorm, from where there is an easy return to the camp site by a forest break road. If the weather is good, most walkers will continue along the ridge with all the time magnificent views of the high Cairngorms. There are three other tops, Creagan Gorm (2,403 feet), an un-named top (2,305 feet), and finally Craig Gowrie (2,237 feet). From either of the latter two, descend, heading for Badaguish. Look for a gate through the deer fence which connects with the route down to Badaguish, and hence back to the camp site.

THE CHALAMAIN GAP

This is one of the several glacial overflow channels and the gap can be seen from the camp site. Follow the ski road to its first bend just beyond the deer fence and cattle grid. Descend to the right, to the bridge over the Allt Mor. A rough path, often very muddy, leads along the burn for about a mile and then strikes upwards towards the gap. The defile in the gap is through and over massed boulders which have fallen down from the crags above, and must be taken carefully, the west wall with much loose rock being for rock climbers only. Once through, the going is easy down to the Lairig Ghru, the Sinclair Mountain Refuge hut being seen on a knoll on the west side of the burn.

The return route is by the Lairig path till one reaches a cross roads in the Rothiemurchus Forest (locally known as Piccadilly). The east branch leads down to the west end of Loch Morlich and the complete round from the camp site is around 11 miles.

EAGLES CORRIE (STAC NA H'IOLAIRE)

Follow the Ryvoan road as far as the fork beyond the Green Loch, then take the branch which leads east, over to the Nethy Hut, called "Bynack Stables" on the Ordnance Survey map. The lochan to the immediate north (Loch a' Gharbh-choire) was at a much higher level last century when it was dam med and wood floated down the Nethy and the Spey to Spey Bay. Don't cross the river at the Nethy Hut, but follow the faint path southwards for about 2 miles, where a burn comes down to join the Nethy from the west. Uphill steeply now, on the south side of the burn. The going through the base of the corries is quite rough and it is much better to keep to the hill on the south till one reaches the southern rim of the corrie. From here one has a fine view of the great cliffs and screes of Stac na h-Iolaire on the north side, where an eagle nested in former times. Note that these cliffs and screes are very loose and dangerous and there should be no attempt to scramble on them should one go through the heart of the corrie.

From the rim of the corrie a route west is not easily picked out, as there is another little corrie to the south. Several return routes are possible. The best route is to head west (and a compass may be required if the mist comes down) over deep heather till one reaches the deer fence. Where the Allt Ban emerges from the forest a stile can be seen—there is much marshy ground around here—and from here a path leads through the woods down to join a forest road. At the forest road, follow the west branch which will lead to the ski road and hence to the camp site. The nesting-boxes for the crested tit can be seen on the way through the forest.

JEAN'S HUT

Before the ski road was built, Jean's Hut was the only building on Coire Cas and was then transferred to Coire an Lochain.

From the car park at the end of the ski road, cross the Allt Mor, curve round the hill side in a south-west direction (there is a faint path)—cross the burn from Coire an t's Sneachda, ascend again and cross over the burn coming down from the lochan at the head of Coire an Lochain. Follow up the burn to the hut which is a short distance below Coire an Lochain. Continue up the coire, surrounded by great cliffs. This is the most impressive of the Cairngorm corries, and snow lingers most of the summer. The most noticeable feature is the huge Red Slab and in winter and spring avalanches roar down here. These cliffs are for mountaineers and rock climbers only, and have been the site of many accidents.

The return journey from the car park is about 4 miles. If no snow remains, Cairn Lochain can be reached by slanting up the ridge to the west of the hut.

CAIRNGORM (4,084 feet)

Cairngorm is now the easiest reached high summit in Scotland—via the car park at the end of the ski road, then by chair lift to the Ptarmigan Restaurant at 3,600 feet, leaving only 400 feet on foot, to reach the cairn. Due to erosion the former direct route from the Ptarmigan is barred, and the indicated path winding round by the east must be followed. This, of course, is the way for the tourists. The real hill walker will gain much more satisfaction by walking all the way from the camp site. Follow the ski road for about 2½ miles, then a huge boulder will be seen on the left—Clach Bharraig (the Foundation Stone indicating, it seems, that it has been there since the flood). Here one joins a well marked path up what is known as the Windy Ridge (Scron an Aonaich on the map). The going is easy all the way to the Ptarmigan and at normal pace the summit can be gained within two hours from the camp site.

This is one of the finest viewpoints in Scotland. Loch Morlich, with its golden sands, glistens below, the valley of Strathspey, the great forests of Glenmore, Rothiemurchus and Abernethy, and in good visibility, away to the north to the bulk of Ben Wyvis. Ben Macdui restricts the view to the south, while Beinn Mheadhoin with its many cairns seems quite near, and below it Loch Etchachan (3,000 feet), the largest lochan at this height in the area, and though frozen over for much of the year, has trout in it. Ben Avon can be seen far to the east, and the mass of Braeriach to the west. Loch Avon itself cannot be seen from the cairn, so deep it lies in the hollow to the south. The rocky outcrop a little way to the east gives a glimpse of the loch and provides shelter from the winds for picnicking.

The descent can be made to the head of Coire Cas and by way of the ridge on its left (Fiacail a Choire Cas), back to the White Lady Shieling. Snow remains here well into the summer and the ridge should be followed for about ½ mile before traversing into the corrie.

In clear weather a favourite route from Cairngorm is by following the edge of the summit plateau round Coire an t'Sneachda to Cairn Lochan, with spectacular rock scenery all the way. From Cairn Lochan continue west, then north to Creag an Leth-choin, "The Lurchers Crag", from where a descent can be made to the path leading up to the Chalamain Gap already described. The story goes that once upon a time in a deer chase a Lurcher dog fell over

67

SOUTH-EAST

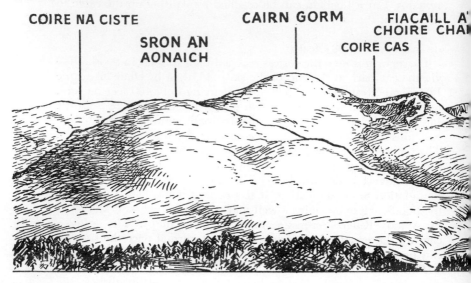

COIRE NA CISTE SRON AN AONAICH CAIRN GORM COIRE CAS FIACAILL A' CHOIRE CHAI

DUE SOUTH

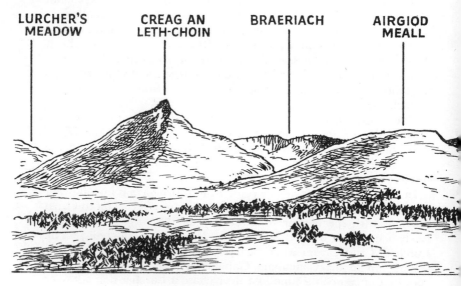

LURCHER'S MEADOW CREAG AN LETH-CHOIN BRAERIACH AIRGIOD MEALL

DUE SOUTH

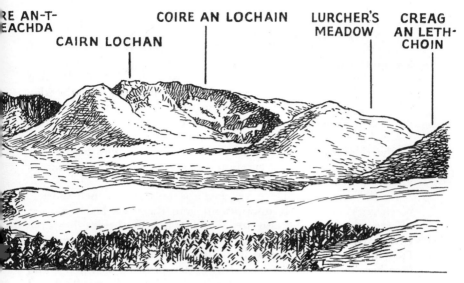

RE AN-T-EACHDA   COIRE AN LOCHAIN   LURCHER'S MEADOW   CREAG AN LETH-CHOIN

CAIRN LOCHAN

SOUTH-WEST

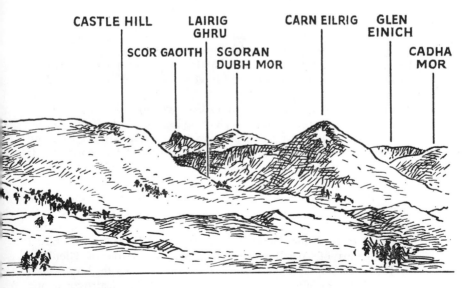

CASTLE HILL   LAIRIG GHRU   CARN EILRIG   GLEN EINICH

SCOR GAOITH   SGORAN DUBH MOR   CADHA MOR

the cliffs here, hence the names applied to the Crag and the Corrie below.

CAIRNGORM BY THE NORTH RIDGE

For the strong hill walker a complete traverse of the mountain—a round of its seven corries—is a most satisfying outing, and very much a good weather route. From the camp site follow the Ryvoan road for almost 2 miles. Just beyond the deer fence marking the edge of the planting and before reaching the Green Loch, a faintly marked path leads steeply uphill starting beside a fire warning notice. Beyond the tree level the route is in a south-east direction to the ridge south of the Eagles Corrie. As one goes higher one notices the changes in vegetation—at first cowberries, blaeberries and deep heather.

By the time the ridge is reached the heather is much shorter, cowberries have mostly disappeared, and there are lovely carpets of creeping azalea and also thrift. This 2-mile long ridge forms the eastern boundary of the park. It is at first broad, featureless and fairly flat, so that a compass is required lest one stray into a corrie. Heather becomes sparse and the flatter growing bearberry and crowberry appear. One passes the head of Corrie Laogh Beag and Coire Laogh Mor (the small and big corries of the calf, indicating where deer used to come when calving). Higher up, near the top, heathers have disappeared altogether and one may find the smallest of our trees, the dwarf willow, and on the tops, carpets of that lovely cushion plant, moss campion.

The ridge leads to what is known as the East Top of Cairngorm, Cnap Coire nan Spreidhe—the lump of the corrie of the antlers. Because of all the ski-ing and lifts, etc., deer are not often seen in these corries, but from this ridge I have seen herds of over a hundred in upper Strath Nethy below to the east, with antlers showing clearly. The corrie between this top and Cairngorm is known as Ciste Mhearad (Margaret's Coffin). Here again we are back in the old days when mentally affected folk were regarded as witches, and one such was driven up the mountain and died there. This corrie holds snow long after others, and in spring is a favourite place for snow-holing practice.

Coire na Ciste itself is the main high level ski-ing area and on the way to the summit of Cairngorm one can visit the Marquis's Well, a spring just 100 feet below and to the north-west of the summit. It is said to be named after the Marquis of Huntly who chased the Marquis of Argyll westwards after the Battle of Glenlivet in 1594. This well is the source of the Allt na Ciste, but is also said to drain through to Margaret's Coffin. From Cairngorm one

70

continues round the corries to the Lurcher's Crag as already described.

BEN MACDUI FROM CAIRNGORM

Ben Macdui, the second highest peak in Scotland, beckons from the summit of Cairngorm. It seems quite near, but the walking distance is about 4 miles, and anyone making the return journey on foot from Glenmore should allow nine hours, or if starting from the upper car park, about six hours. A direct route from Cairngorm is not possible. One can either go round the corries to Cairn Lochan from where Lochan Buidhe (the Yellow Loch) can be seen, or take a compass bearing on the latter and a direct route which crosses the upper parts of Coire Raibeirt and Coire Domhain. By this route one does not see the lochan till almost reaching it, so compass work should be accurate.

From the lochan, the dividing point between Cairngorm and Ben Macdui the route is almost due south. This is all quite easy in clear weather as the going is over gravel and sand with rocks and boulders here and there, while there are cairns from the lochan. Many parties, however, have lost themselves on this plateau through being without map or compass, or ability to use either properly, when mist comes down. Be sure and obtain the morning weather forecast for this journey and turn back if bad weather arises.

Of all the peaks of the Cairngorms none commands such wide spread views as Macdui. On a clear day the visibility north to south is almost 200 miles, and from east to west over 100 miles— a veritable sea of mountains all round and the indicator on the summit will help you to pick them out. Most impressive is that to the immediate west, the tremendous rocky amphitheatre from Braeriach to Cairntoul in whose upper corries the snow often lies the whole year round.

The return journey can be by the Yellow Loch, then round Cairn Lochan to the Lurcher's Corrie, or to Coire Cas and descent by Fiacall a' Choire Cas, both routes already mentioned.

BYNACK MORE (3,574 feet)

This mountain is well worth visiting and has the most notable tors of all the Cairngorm peaks. Take the road to the Nethy Hut where the Lairig an Laoigh path starts across the bridge. The gradient is easy and the path well marked. At its highest point, head direct south and follow the ridge, the upper part of it consisting of a series of rocky knobs like vertebrae with a route for the scrambler over them or a route round them. The scenic tors known as the Barns of Bynack can't be seen from the summit and are about 300 feet to the south-east. There are three masses varying in height from 50 to 100 feet, the impressive rock sculpture calling for photographs. A return is best made by the outward route and involves in all about 15 miles.

BRAERIACH (4,248 feet)

From Aviemore this peak, the third highest in Scotland, with its great north facing corries, appears much more impressive than Cairngorm and always carries more snow. It might well have been developed for ski-ing had access facilities been available. It is best approached by the Lairig Ghru. The traditional start of this path is at Coylumbridge, 2 miles from Aviemore, then 2 miles on the west bank of the burn to the Cairngorm Club bridge, then gradually rising and emerging from the forest with a flattish section till opposite the Sinclair Hut. This part of the route was formerly mostly a mud bath, but recently much improved by the good work of the Conservation Corps. From the hut the ascent is made up the long shoulder of Sron na Lairig to a height of 3,860 feet.

Beyond this the way descends a little to a col at 3,700 feet, from where the route to the summit is westwards above the great corries of Braeriach's northern flank. Not many yards from the cairn the hillside plunges over into Coire Bhrochain in a sheer wall of crag; beyond it lies an almost 2 mile stretch of continuous crag which rims the huge neighbouring recess of Garbh Choire. A return can be made to the col already mentioned, from where one can descend by a steep stalkers' path to the Lairig and have a look at the Pools of Dee. There are three pools in all, almost symmetrical in shape and paved with stones which makes them look almost artificial. The stream connecting the Pools runs underground, appears further down the Pass and flows to join the Dee.

The summit of the Pass is just a little way north of the Pools at a height of 2,733 feet, and the path followed to join the outward route opposte the Sinclair Hut.

LOCH AVON AND THE SHELTER STONE

Loch Avon, at a height of 2,377 feet and two miles long, cannot be seen from the summit of either Cairngorm or Ben Macdui. Up till recent years it was about the most inaccessible and remote loch in Scotland with a long, hard trek in any direction to reach it. Now, with the Cairngorm Ski Road and Chairlift, the approach from the north is much shorter and the loch has many more visitors than formerly.

From the summit of Cairngorm descend south to upper Coire Raibeirt

Plate 38. A climber on the "Savage Slit".

Plate 39. The Fiacaill Ridge above the Coire Cas.

Plate 40. On the Cairngorm Plateau. Looking west from Cairngorm summit towards the Lurcher's Crag over the barren tundra-like wastes. Coire Cas, right, is a typical glaciated hollow. The distant mountain is Braeriach, beyond the Lairig Ghru.

Plate 41.   Cairn Lochan Cliffs.

Plate 42.   Ice axes in action.

Plate 43. Climbing practice on the training tower at Glenmore Lodge.

Plate 44.   Ascent of an ice face.

Plate 45. Helicopter rescue practice: winching up.

Plate 46. Rescue party practice crossing river.

Plate 47. A helicopter touches down to pick up a casualty.

Plate 48.   Climbers on the Barns of Bynack.

—the opposite side of the mountain from Coire Cas. This at first is a wide depression and mostly muddy and wet where the stream starts. Lower down the corrie becomes steep and narrow. The going at first is on the east side, then crosses over to the west side at a steep section from where the path descends and curves round to the head of the loch. The other approach to Coire Raibeirt is from the Shieling by a rough path to Fiacall a Choire Cas to the cairn at its head, and then as formerly. This approach gives a magnificent view of the head of the loch with its encircling crags, the waters of Feith Bhuidhe and Garbh Uisge tumbling down and snow remaining often in July.

To reach Loch Avon from Cairn Lochan the descent is by Coire Domhain (the steep corrie) keeping to the east side of the burn. Both descents should be taken carefully and are slippery in wet weather.

The Shelter Stone is a huge boulder, almost the size of a small cottage, which at some remote time has fallen down from the cliffs above to come to rest on a smaller boulder, leaving a natural refuge between them. It can be easily picked out with a cairn on its top. Its first written mention is in the Statistical Account of Scotland of 1794—"Close by Lochavon there is a large stone called Cladh-dhain from Clach, a stone, and Dhain, a protection or refuge . . . it has a cavity within, capable of holding 18 armed men. In times of licence and depredation, it offered a retreat for free-booters". The stone is also mentioned in Sir Thomas Dick Lauder's novel *The Wolf of Badenoch*, published in 1827. Its accommodation is over-emphasised in these early accounts and ten lying down inside is a bit of a crush. Crevices have been filled up with stones and turf. It is not entirely windproof but rainproof except under very heavy rain, when there may be a drip at the rear. It is quite dark inside but with stoves going and candles flickering it is a very cheery haven. Many famous folk have visited it, including former Prime Ministers Gladstone and Ramsay Macdonald, so that it is rightly claimed as the Mecca of Scottish hill walkers. From 1924 when the Cairngorm Club installed a visitors' book, records have been kept, and these, now in Aberdeen, tell its story.

In war time the Cairngorm mountains were a training ground for Commandos before the invasion of Europe. Polish troops, Norwegian troops and soldiers from a great many British regiments entered their names proudly in the book.

In the summer the Shelter is often crowded out. Other shelters have been made under nearby boulders while uphill a bit is a huge open cave which is also used, but not quite rain proof. The com-

73

paratively easy access via Chair Lift has led to a great increase in rock climbing in the area, the Shelter Stone Crag offering climbs of the most severe standard.

THE SADDLE—STRATH NETHY

For a day visitor descending by Coire Raibeirt the return can be made via Coire Domhain or *vice versa*. A longer return route is via the Saddle. One retraces the route as far as the burn coming down from Coire Raibeirt from where a loch side track is followed for another mile then winds up 300 feet to the pass between Cairngorm and A' Choineach. Across the pass the route goes north by the Garbh Allt (the upper water of the Nethy) with Bynack Mor on the east, and finishes at the Nethy Hut from where the road is followed to Glenmore. This route is known as the escape route from Loch Avon in bad weather, as it is comparatively sheltered.

LOCH ETCHACHAN

Many will want to bivouac overnight under the Shelter Stone and there are trout in Loch Avon. For such a two day journey, a return can be made over Ben Macdui. From the Stone a steep path leads up under the crags of Cairn Etchachan to Loch Etchachan at the east end of which one joins the path from Glen Derry, with about 2 miles from here circling round to the summit and return with routes already described. But always remember the sudden weather changes, and perhaps a better way would be to take Macdui on the outward journey when one can have the weather report that morning, leaving the easier journey back should the weather change. Beann Mheadhoin can be easily climbed from Loch Etchachan, ascending and descending directly from the loch.

THE HILL PASSES

The following three routes describe mountain passes which link Speyside with Deeside.

LAIRIG GHRU (*The Forbidding Pass*)

The Lairig Ghru is the best known and finest of the Cairngorm passes, taking one into the very heart of the range and rising at its highest point to 2,733 feet. The usual start is from Coylumbridge as far as the Sinclair Hut. From the camp site at Glenmore the approach can be made as far as the cross-roads in the forest or via Chalamain Gap. South of the Sinclair Hut the path climbs steadily to a maze of boulders at its highest point. As one descends past the Pools of Dee, the Garbh Choire, where snow ever lingers, looms up to the west with the shapely peak of the Devil's Point far to the south.

Continuing south over the rough path one crosses the Allt Clach nan Taillear (the burn of the tailor's stone). According to the story, once three tailors wagered that they would dance a reel on the same night in Rothiemurchus and Braemar, and, having danced in Speyside, set out through the Lairig, were overtaken by bad weather at this point and all three died in the snow—all this at New Year time. Just about a mile further south, the Corrour Bothy can be seen on the other side of the Dee, and it is worth crossing over the bridge to visit it and rest there. After that the path climbs uphill, round the shoulder of Carn a' Mhaim to Luibeg and Derry Lodge, from where there is a private road to Inverey and then public road to Braemar.

On a tablet in a parapet of Cairngorm Footbridge the distances and approximate times are given as follows:

To Aviemore	4 miles	1½ hours
To Coylumbridge	2 miles	¾ hour
To Summit of Pass	5½ miles	3 hours
To Derry Lodge	14 miles	6½ hours
To Linn of Dee	18 miles	8 hours
To Braemar	24½ miles	10 hours

Of above, 11 miles are roads, and the remainder paths.

LAIRIG AN LAOIGH (*The Pass of the Calves*)

If one has to return to Speyside after travelling through the Lairig Ghru, overnight accommodation can be had at Inverey or Braemar (Youth Hostels at both), with return by this much less known and less used pass. The route as far as Derry Lodge is the same. From there the path runs north for 2 miles through ancient pine forest to Derry Dam. There is a new steel bridge here and another across the Glass Allt 2 miles further on. A little way on, the path to Ben Macdui goes up Coire Etchachan to the west, while the Lairig path continues north between Beinn a Chaorruinn and Bheinn Mheadhoin to reach the River Avon at a ford called Ath na Fiann, indicating association with the legendary Celtic warrior Fingal. There are no bothies on this route but a rude emergency shelter on the north side of the river.

For some miles north of the ford the route is fairly flat, first winding between Creag Mhor and A' Choinneach, then round the slopes of Bynack Mor and, if clear, the Barns of Bynack can be seen. The path after crossing the upper tributaries of the River Caiplich at two points, ascends north-west to its highest point at 2,536 feet, and crosses a flat featureless plateau before descending to the valley of the Nethy at Nethy Hut. The plateau is very exposed with no shelter whatever, and though there are cairns it is all too easy to stray from the path.

75

There are records of parties losing themselves on this route, and wandering down the Caiplich to find themselves ultimately at Tomintoul. At Easter 1960 two hill walkers lost their lives when a snow storm blew up.

Distances

Aviemore	to	Camp Site	7 miles	Public road
Camp Site	to	Nethy Hut	4 miles	Forest road
Nethy Hut	to	Ford of Avon	6 miles	Path
Ford of Avon	to	Derry Lodge	7 miles	Path
Derry Lodge	to	Braemar	10½ miles	Road
		Total	34½ miles	

GELDIE—FESHIE PASS

An alternative return route from Inverey could be by this historic route, planned as a road by General Wade 200 years ago, suggested many times since, but not yet built. Only 9 miles, however, is entirely road-less. Two miles from Inverey is the Linn of Dee where the river rushes through a narrow channel and then opens out into a series of great circular pools. Continuing, one reaches White Bridge at the junction of the Dee and the Geldie, and where the Dee turns north. The track keeps to the north side of the Geldie, the glen being featureless and desolate, though in Victorian times a mansion house existed on the south side of the river, 5 miles from White Bridge. West of this the track is poorly marked and one should look for cairns leading uphill quite away from the river.

The bealach between the Geldie and the Feshie is quite low, rising only to 1,850 feet and to the junction of the Eideart with the Feshie. No attempt should be made to ford the Eidart at its mouth (a hill walker was drowned while attempting to do so). Look for a new bridge a little way upstream. All downhill after this, with the great forests of Speyside in the distance. Entering the forest, a rough road has been bulldozed recently along the Great Screes, descending again through ancient pines to Glen Feshie Lodge where the river turns north. In the heart of the forest here is what is now called the Landseer Hut, a building built over the ruins of a cottage where that great painter lived in Queen Victoria's time while making many of his famous paintings.

From the Lodge there is a private road for 2 miles where one crosses a wooden bridge to the public road at Achlean. The whole distance from Inverey to Achlean is 21 miles and another 12 miles to Aviemore, first to Feshie Bridge, then by the old road on the east bank of the Spey.

The ascent of the four peaks over 4,000 feet high, Cairngorm, Ben Macdui, Cairntoul and Braeriach in one day is a classic major expedition and for settled weather in summer only. It is advisable also that those intending to do so have previous knowledge of ascents of the four peaks. A 6 a.m. start is not too early, as the average strong hill walker will take about 12 hours, possibly more.

Some may want to cover the long trek to Braeriach first, while others will prefer to gain height early on and start with Cairngorm. The round trip, camp site to camp site, is about 22 miles of very rough hill walking with about 7,000 feet of ascent, though this can be cut down if one has transport to the Ski Road car park. From the car park Cairngorm can be reached well within one hour, then take the previously described route to Ben Macdui. From there the usual route is to descend by Tailor's Burn (2,000 feet) to the Lairig Ghru, and thence to Corrour Bothy—(and turn back via Lairig should the weather break). From Corrour a path leads up and circles round the cliffs to Cairntoul.

From here on a clear day the going is easy, a desert of gravel and sand and much of it above 4,000 feet; but in mist very, very careful navigation is required, walking almost 2 miles west and judging according to one's pace when to turn and head north to reach the Wells of Dee, the real source of the river, from where there is a gentle rise of about 300 feet to the summit of Braeriach. From here, the best return is via Sron na Lairig and the Sinclair Hut.

*   *   *   *

From these journeys into the Cairngorm Mountains the visitor will depart with an unforgettable appreciation of their grandeur and variety, the high plateaux, summits, crags, remote glens, corries, lochans and ancient Caledonia.

Where essential silence chills and blesses
And for ever in the hill recesses
Her more lovely music broods and dies . . .
For there among the flowers and grasses
Only the mightier movement sounds and passes,
Only winds and rivers, life and death.

— Stevenson

The Leader

And now, tensed, balanced, gripping, holding
My weight down to the centre of ledge then ledge
Which it takes one step to remove—
Just shifting my treacherous strength
To make a fulcrum of nothing.

— Paul Mills

THE CLIMBING GROUNDS
OF THE PARK

By Eric Langmuir and John Cunningham

The Cairngorm mountains have a reputation for remoteness which is borne out by the fact that, even today, the full development of their climbing potential has not been realised. They have also suffered, or been protected, depending on your viewpoint, by a reputation for poor, somewhat vegetated rock. It is perfectly true that on some crags this generalisation applies, as it does to almost any extensive mountain range, but the Cairngorms are no worse and no better than most and some magnificent rock climbing is available for the discerning visitor. The rock is a rough pink granite, sculptured by the high glaciers of past ice ages into impressive corries, ringed by crags. These vary enormously in structure, depending on the exposure and the degree of shattering, from impressive sheets of slabs to steep pinnacled walls, but in general, the rock is somewhat massive in character and rounded by the effects of weathering. The net result of this is that the climbing tends to be rather more difficult than appears at first sight.

In winter-time the whole range is transformed. No other group of mountains in Britain offers such reliable conditions for the snow and ice climber. There is a fairly heavy snow fall, usually packed by the ubiquitous wind into the gullies, chimneys and coire head walls, where it lies well into the month of May. Indeed, there are isolated patches of snow which have not melted for many years, though this is more properly attributed to the low mean summer temperatures. Since the cliffs fringe the plateau they tend to be high and this is yet another factor which favours the retention of the snow.

The greatest phase of development in the history of climbing in the Cairngorms came in the fifties and, in the area covered by this guide, a great deal of activity centred round Glenmore Lodge, the Outdoor Training Centre opened by the Central Council of Physical Recreation in 1949. The building of the ski-road and the Cairngorm chairlift has stimulated another phase of exploration, bringing all the crags of the Loch Avon horseshoe within two hours of Glenmore. However, in spite of this improved access, from a climbing point of view, the Cairngorms remain one of the least developed mountain areas in the country.

On a fine summer's day it is easy to be misled by the rolling hills and the ease with which it is possible to traverse them. They are aptly called "the hill-walker's paradise" and yet they can also be the hill-walker's graveyard. The very lack of features which make hill-walking so painless puts a premium on the ability to use map and compass when the mist comes down. The Cairngorm mountains probably get less bad weather than any other comparable range in Britain, but when they do, it can be very bad. The extensive high-level plateau can be a trap for the unwary or unprepared, flanked as it is by steep coire walls and exposed to the full blast of the wind and rain. The temperature, too, is up to 10° Centigrade colder than at Aviemore and this means that, even at the height of summer, storms of snow and hail can occur. (To illustrate what this implies, Plate 34, showing strollers in sun dresses in Glen More Forest, was taken on the same April afternoon as Plate 56, showing well-clad skiers on the snows near Cairngorm summit.) If these remarks are true in summer they are doubly so in winter. Even the most cursory of glances at the accident record for the area reveals that faulty navigation and slips on hard snow, usually in descent, are two of the most important contributory factors. The inability to arrest a slide once started is obviously another.

Old-fashioned nailed boots or vibrams with well-fitting crampons should be the order of the winter day. The ferocity of the Cairngorm blizzard is legendary, and climbers would do well to pay close attention to the weather forecast, suitably amended to take account of the increases in wind speed and decrease in temperature due to altitude. A less obvious hazard, but one to which the snow and ice climber is particularly exposed, is the winter avalanche. (Plates 11 and 12). It can take many forms, but there is no doubt that the greatest danger is from the soft slab avalanche which falls during, or immediately after, heavy snow fall. In the Cairngorms these avalanches are normally associated with the build-up of heavy masses of snow transported by the wind and are therefore common on head walls and open lee-slopes. Climbers should take particular care in approaching climbs across snow-covered scree slopes or rock slabs such as are found in Coire an Lochan. Perhaps more obvious, but no less real, is the risk of cornice collapse. This is most frequent in thaw conditions when there is more widespread danger of wet slab slides from old crust layers on smooth rock.

It can not be too strongly emphasised that the general description which follows of the climbing possibilities in the Forest Park is not a substitute for a guide book. Readers are referred to the excellent guide produced by the Scottish Mountaineering Club, *Climber's Guide to the Cairngorms Area*, Volume I: *Loch Avon Horseshoe Northern Corries*, and to John Cunningham's *Guide to Winter Climbs (Selected) Cairngorms and Creag Meaghaidh*. Of the eight cliffs described here, only four fall wholly within the Forest Park area: Coire an-t-Sneachda, Coire an Lochan, and the minor crags, Creag a' Chalamain and Creagan Dubh. The others are so closely related to these, both in terms of access and geographical position, that it would be misleading to exclude them. Each crag is treated separately with a comprehensive description of how to get there, and a general description of the main features and peculiarities of the cliff in summer and winter conditions. Two or three routes are recommended for those who are new to the area. Those selected are of a fairly modest standard of difficulty and are among the best climbs which that particular cliff has to offer. The gradings referred to are those in current use in the Scottish Mountaineering Club guides, ranging from Very Severe to Moderate, and a numerical grading for snow and ice routes, ranging from 5 to 1, one being the easiest classification.

The numerals refer to the National Grid, as printed on all Ordnance Survey Maps.

CREAGAN DUBH (CRANBERRY ROCKS), COIRE NA CISTE, NJ001070

Take the Cairngorm road to the road junction NH991075. Follow the left fork to the Coire Na Ciste car park. From the car park go south for two hundred yards or so, then descend gently to the Allt na Ciste. Cross the stream and continue up the path on the East bank until directly beneath the crag. Climb steeply up to the lower rocks.

Time—20 minutes.

There is a wide variety of short rock climbs on the Creagan Dubh crags, ranging from difficult slabs to some very steep, very severe cracks and walls. A useful practice area, but great care should be exercised when using this crag as there is a very real danger of falling stones, especially when other parties are climbing.

COIRE AN T'SNEACHDA, NH995032

From the South end of the car park cross the wooden bridge over the Allt a Choire Chais, to join the footpath which follows the contours west-wards, then S.S.W. to the ford at the Allt Coire an-t-Sneachda. Follow the burn S.S.E. by a rough, poorly-defined track to its source a few hundred yards N.E. of the lochans in the coire floor. Clamber over the boulder field to the lochans beneath the cliffs.

2 miles, 1,000ft. of ascent. Time—1½ hours.

An alternative route is to take the chairlift to the White Lady Shieling and follow the Fiacaill a Choire Chais ski tow to the ridge. An indistinct path follows the contours round into Coire an t'Sneachda, descending gently towards the lochans.

1 mile 700 yards, 550 feet of ascent. Time—1 hour.

Coire an t'Sneachda is really two coires merged into one, the smaller of the two lying in the S.W. corner. It is bounded on the East by the Fiacaill a Choire Chais, and on the West by the Fiacaill Coire an-t-Sneachda, usually referred to as the Fiacaill Ridge. The crags comprise a series of generally rather broken rock buttresses with a great deal of unstable rock, separated by gullies which in winter time, offer a good variety of climbs in the Grade I-II range.

From the summit the easiest way back into the Coire is via the goat track which descends from the Col at the head of Coire Domhain (steep, straightforward snow, easy Grade I in winter). If returning to the car park, follow the edge of the Coire round to the N.E., and descend by the Fiacaill a Choire Chais. The N.E. side of this ridge is steep and sometimes corniced in winter. Keep well to the West going down.

COIRE AN LOCHAN, NH983027

From the Car Park follow the route described as far as the Allt Coire an t'Sneachda. Cross the burn and continue on this path for a further 700 yards (to where the path begins to level off). Turn southwards at this point (981046) and walk over easy terrain to reach Jean's hut approximately 1 mile further on. Continue on a southwards bearing to reach the lochans below the cliffs of Coire an Lochan.

2 miles 700 yards, 1,000 feet of ascent. Time—1½ hours.

Coire an Lochan is altogether a more impressive Coire than its neighbour and more serious from a climbing point of view. A unique feature of the Coire is the great apron of smooth granite slabs which lie below the upper buttresses. Set at a relatively easy angle, these slabs act as a chute for some really major avalanches, particularly in the spring, when percolating melt water loosens the attachment between snow and rock. At this time of year the Central Slabs should be avoided as an approach to the crags.

In summer there are few climbs which can be recommended at or below very difficult standard with the exception of Savage Slit, a firm, steep, crack line on Number 4 buttress. Harder climbs of up to 350 feet in length abound.

In winter conditions the Coire retains its serious character and though there are climbs of all grades of difficulty they nearly all involve an approach either across, or above, the Great Slab.

There are no easy ways from the summit back down into the Coire and one must either descend by the Fiacaill Ridge just to the east of the summit Cairn, or by the west rim of the Coire until it is possible to descend directly to the Lochan, keeping to the north side of the stream which runs into it. If taking this latter route in winter it is well to remember that the plateau is deeply incised by gullies in several places and in most it is necessary to give the edge a wide berth.

CREAG A' CHALAMAIN, NH966053

Follow the Cairngorm road to the bend just south of the forest boundary fence. A well defined path is followed down to the bridge, crossing the Allt Mor at NH984071. Cross the bridge and continue up-stream for just over 1 mile to the ford at 973063. Cross the ford and follow the broad muddy path south west to the Chalamain Gap, an old melt water channel.

2 miles, 300 yards, 750 feet of ascent. Time—1 hour 10 minutes.

It is also possible to approach the crag more or less due west from the car park, skirting the boggy ground between the Sneachda and Lochan burns.

This is an excellent training area offering a great variety of short, 1-pitch climbs on rough sound granite. All of the rock climbing is situated on the 6 small buttresses on the right (N.W.) side of the gap, and the standard of the routes range from easy to hard severe.

CREAG AN LETHCHOIN, NH968034

Follow the path as for the route to the Chalamain Gap. Go through the gap and immediately contour towards the south, following the hillside without losing height to the bottom of Lurcher's Crag, overlooking the Lairig Ghru, E.S.E. from the Sinclair Hut.

4 miles, 300 yards, 800 feet of ascent, Time—2 hours.

No climbs have been recorded on Creag an Lethchoin in summer. However, under winter conditions it offers good practice slopes for ice climbing.

Recommended Routes

Summer	.	. None	
Winter	.	. North Gully	800 ft. (Grade II–III)

From the summit it is best to return by the Allt Creag an Lethchoin and follow the contours easily round to the Cairngorm car park.

STAC AN FHARAIDH, NJ012030

From the top station of the Cairngorm chairlift follow the new Cairngorm summit track for about 500 yards until it swings south. Descend S.E. to the Strath Nethy Saddle. The Stac an Fharaidh slabs are on a level with the Saddle overlooking Loch Avon, some 500 yards to the S.W.

1½ miles. Time—½ hour.

A splendid sweep of south-facing slabs overlooking Loch Avon offering climbs up to 500 feet in length. The slabs are divided into east and west flanks by a broad gulley and are interrupted by over-laps and a final wall which provides much of the climbing interest with standards ranging from difficult to hard, very severe. No winter climbs have been recorded and it is obvious from the nature

83

of the rock that there is a real danger of slab avalanches, particularly in the spring.

From the summit of Stac an Fharaidh Slabs the most direct route back lies to the N.W., traversing the east side of Coire Raibeirt and descending by the Fiacaille a Choire Chais.

Recommended Routes

Summer . .	Pipit Slab	460 ft. (very difficult)
	Après Moi	500 ft. (severe)
	Rectangular Rib	270 ft. (difficult)

STAGROCKS, NJ001021

From the White Lady Shieling take the line of the Fiacaill ski tow up to the ridge. Follow the path up the well-defined Fiacaill a Choire Chais to its summit.

Descend by the east bank of the Allt Choire Raibeirt. This route is gently angled at first, then plunges steeply towards Loch Avon. Half way down the steep section a traverse to the S.W. takes one easily to the bottom of Stagrocks.

In winter, after heavy snow fall, there is no safe way into the Loch Avon trough from the north, other than by the Strath Nethy Saddle. Both Coire Raibeirt and Coire Domhain are prone to avalanche.

2 miles, 1,000 yards, 1,235 feet of axcent. Time—1½ hours.

Stagrocks consist of a line of south facing crags at the W. end of Loch Avon opposite the Shelter Stone crag. Together with the adjoining Stac an Fharaidh, these cliffs offer a variety of climbs of a less serious nature than their neighbours across the valley.

Recommended Routes:

Summer . .	Quartz Diggers'	
	Cave Route	250 ft. (very difficult)
	Pine Tree Route	500 ft. (difficult)
	The Tenements	500 ft. (very difficult)
Winter . .	Diagonal Gully	600 ft. (Grade I)

HELL'S LUM CRAG, NH996018

From the White Lady Sheiling follow the previous route to the summit of the Fiacaill a Choire Chais.

From here take the path round the edge of Coire an t'Sneachda and up to the cairn at its summit. Descend to the source of the Allt Coire Domhain and follow the stream down to where it suddenly steepens.

Go down a very steep path for about 500 feet until an easy traverse to the south leads to the bottom of the crag.

2 miles, 130 yards, 1,500 feet of ascent. Time—1 hour, 45 minutes.

84

In winter it is important to remember that the same reservations about access after heavy snow fall apply to this crag as to the others on the north side of Loch Avon. In fact the whole slope between the Allt Coire Domhain and the Garbh Uisge is prone to avalanche.

Hell's Lum is a very impressive 500 feet compact crag at the west end of the Loch Avon trough, between the Allt Coire Domhain and the Feith Buidhe. The rock is a sound, massive granite offering many fine routes in the middle grades of difficulty. The crag gets its name from the deep cleft near the south end which separates the main cliff from an area of steep slabs.

Recommended Routes:

Summer	.	.	Kiwi Slabs	450 ft. (very difficult)
			Deep Cut Chimney	500 ft. (very difficult)
Winter	.	.	Escalator	400 ft. (Grade II–III)
			Hell's Lum	500 ft. (Grade II–III)

MAP REFERENCES OF BOTHIES AND REFUGES

Ryvoan	NJ006115	One-roomed stone cottage
Nethy Bothy	NJ020105	Corrugated iron stable
Alamein Hut*	NJ016053	Stone, covered refuge, difficult to find in winter
St. Valery's Refuge*	NJ002022	Stone, covered refuge at top of Stag Rocks (orange marker)
Curran Bothy*	NH983010	Stone, covered refuge at south end of Lochan Bhuidhe
Sinclair Hut	NH959037	Small two-roomed stone building
Jean's Hut	NH981034	Wooden hut, with one room and front porch
Shelter Stone	NJ002016	Situated beneath the largest boulder under Shelter Stone Crag (cairn on top)

*Due for demolition and resiting in 1974

REFERENCES

Maps:

    O.S., 1 inch to 1 mile, Sheet 38, *Grantown and Cairngorm*
    O.S., 1 inch to 1 mile, Tourist Edition, *The Cairngorms*
    O.S., 1 : 25000, Outdoor Leisure Map: *High Tops of the Cairngorms*

Scottish Mountaineering Club:
    Climber's Guide to the Cairngorms Area:
    Volume I, Loch Avon Horseshoe, Northern Corries
    Guide to Winter Climb—Cairngorms and Creag Meaghaidh:
    by JOHN CUNNINGHAM (selected routes)

Off to the Hills

GLENMORE LODGE
THE NATIONAL
OUTDOOR TRAINING CENTRE

By F. W. J. Harper, *Principal, Glenmore Lodge*

Glenmore Lodge, situated near the eastern border of the Park, is operated by the Scottish Sports Council which assumed responsibility on the dissolution of the Scottish Council of Physical Recreation in 1972.

The Scottish Sports Council is, by Royal Charter, charged with the encouragement of participation in all sports, and at all levels, amongst the people of Scotland. In pursuing this aim in respect of the so-called Outdoor Activities, sometimes called Adventure Activities, the Council operates Glenmore Lodge as an establishment providing residential training in the following sports: Rock Climbing, Mountaineering, Snow and Ice Climbing, Ski-ing, White Water Canoeing, Sailing, and Field Studies.

When in 1947 the Lodge first began to operate, courses were mostly for schoolchildren and for adults who wished to take up

86

climbing, sailing or whatever other sport attracted them. However the work of the Lodge has changed over the years and most courses now planned are for those who are already skilled in one of the activities, but who wish to be trained, and in due course certificated, as instructors in the activities concerned. Much of the work currently done is therefore at a high technical level and is aimed directly at the producing increasing numbers of outdoor activity instructors who will, in their employment as teachers, youth leaders or simply as interested willing and proficient individuals, interest increasing numbers of young people in one or other of the outdoor pursuits available amid these mountains.

A number of courses listed in a brochure published every six months, are still held each year for those adults who simply wish to take up one of the outdoor activities themselves. These Skills Training Courses are very popular indeed and are important because it is essential that novices in the "risk Sports" establish a sound basis of safe technique and approach. Each Skills Training Course sets out to teach the safest practice, whether on a rock face or on the rapids of our rivers.

Two courses each year are held for schoolchildren who wish to become hill-walkers, canoeists, or sailors, or in winter, skiers. These courses are very popular and enjoyable but early booking is essential if a place is required. The age limits in this group are 14 years to 17 years inclusive.

A number of other courses are run each year for adults. For instance, there is a course of training in Mountain Rescue techniques, primarily for those who are, or who aspire to be, members of mountain rescue teams. This is generally held in October. Also there is, each year in winter, our Survival course, to train in winter survival those who find their pleasure on high mountains or amidst arctic conditions.

Quite a few "sampling" courses are held for educational establishments who ask us to arrange courses for them, particularly the Colleges of Physical Education. These courses aim to introduce each student to each of the activities, allowing an educated valid choice, regarding actual participation, to be made at the end of the sampling course. For those who choose positively further opportunities for training are then generally made available.

The work of the Lodge, clearly, is diverse within certain limits. The aim is equally clear, to affect the leisure and recreation habits of the people of Scotland by the provision of opportunity to participate in, and to learn the basics of, new activities in the splendid outdoors provided by the Cairngorm area and particularly the Glenmore Forest Park.

Further information about courses available to individual members of the public and to organisations is available from:

THE SECRETARY,		THE PRINCIPAL,
Scottish Sports Council	*or*	Glenmore Lodge,
4 Queensferry Street,		Aviemore,
Edinburgh EH4 2PB		Highlands

Plate 49. The Cairngorm Plateau under snow seen from the summit of Cairngorm. The far peaks, to the west beyond the Lairig Ghru, are Cairn Toul, left, Einich Cairn, and misty Braeriach.

Plate 50. Drifting snow on the Cairngorm Plateau.

Plate 51. Beginner's Class.

Plate 52. Advanced Ski-ing.

Plate 53.   Ski-jumping: going up.

Plate 54.   Ski-jumping: coming down.

Plate 55.   Cairngorm ski lift and the White Lady Shieling.

Plate 56.   The Ptarmigan ski tow.

Plate 57. The car park ski tow.

Plate 58. The Norwegian Hostel.

Plate 59. Glen More Lodge.

Plate 60. Woodland car park and picnic seats.

Plate 61. Pinewood camp site.

Plate 62.　West End Car Park. A springtime view through the pines, across Loch Morlich, to snow-wreathed Cairngorm.

Plate 63.　Glenmore Caravan Park.

High on Cairngorm

Space of an amplitude gigantic fashioned our mountains and forest,
Moulding corries in the gray crags for the knuckles of the wind,
Spreading slopes of heather and the bristling pine . . .

— William Jeffrey

SKI-ING IN THE CAIRNGORMS

By Douglas Allan Godlington

As the highest landmass in the whole of the British Isles, the Cairngorms occupy a special geographic position. Not only are there several peaks and large areas of ground above 4,000 feet, but their location ensures that the winter snows collect and stay long enough to provide the best ski-ing conditions in Britain. The huge rounded shapes and terrain of these mountains, as compared to the more craggy and broken shapes of other Scottish hills, lends itself to innumerable downhill runs in overall snowcover.

These mountains are akin to the Arctic lands on the high plateau, and as such should never be treated lightly, especially if a tour away from the popular areas is contemplated. Viewed from Aviemore, the Cairngorms rise from the wide expanse of glen and forest, sheltered ground where only for a few weeks snow can lie to a foot or so depth. It is not until the slopes have climbed to above the tree-line and on to the 2,000 feet contour, that a sudden change

89

occurs. This is where there is a dramatic alteration in the climate, snow collects and remains above this level for six months in the year, falling in storms and gales to fill the corries. These Arctic storms drift and fill the time-aged gullies and folds in the hills with snow, sometimes to a considerable depth. Even though over this huge area of high ground the average total winter snowfall is not excessive, any precipitation that occurs between October and May is likely to fall as snow.

The severe winter storms and winds are both the friend and enemy of the skier. The corries and watercourses fill in with ten to thirty feet of snowdepth to form natural ski runs, unlike the Alps where a thick overall layer of snow forms a ski-ing base. The variable weather pattern which the British Isles "enjoys" helps the ski-ing possibilities by collecting the snows and depositing them into specific drifted areas on the mountains. Some of these snowbeds are a regular feature, immediately recognizable by their shape when seen from the Glen More approaches. Coire Cas forms into a long scimitar shape, and the White Lady snow is self-explanatory. Other snowbeds appear one year and may not reappear for the next year or two, depending on the direction from which the main snow-bearing winds have originated.

The prevailing south-westerly winds and gales drift large masses of snow on to slopes and gullies of a northerly aspect, which in the case of Cairngorm is most of the ski terrain. However, winter storms out of the north-west and other compass points can produce sub-stantial areas of deep skiable snow for much of the season. Fortunately the location of the Cairngorm region, in the east-central part of the Grampians, protects the lying snows to some extent from the warm moist air streams that occur from the western seaboard. The mountains of the west coast of Scotland provide a kind of barricade that help to dry out and cool the warm weak fronts that are part of our weather scene. With easterly weather conditions very dry and frosty days are common, and clear blue skies with very low temperatures produce weather and snow conditions similar to the continent.

SNOW CONDITIONS

The snow that is packed deep into the corries forms into a very durable ski-ing base. Wind and weather consolidate the layers into a high-density mass, ageing quickly into the characteristic crystals of "spring snow" that can withstand sudden thaws and winter climatic frustrations. Although after a storm the newly-packed snow can be formed into waves and ridges as thick slabs, that are difficult to ski over. On the main ski runs the irregular surface of windslab is quickly broken down to give excellent ski-ing, but care must be taken when ski-ing away from the patrolled areas especially if the slope is steep, as windslab snow is the main cause of avalanches in the Cairngorms. A lee slope at the head of a sheltered corrie can accumulate a mass of slab snow in one storm, and may be unstable for a long period afterwards, until the normal weathering process has been able to consolidate the underlying snowlayers.

At the beginning of the season, from the beginning of December onwards, the main snowbeds are forming, sometimes quickly and in some seasons gradually drifting in to widen the ski-ing base. Snow does appear in October most years and gives good ski-ing on the upper levels, but as no base has had time to form, a warm westerly can wipe the hills clear again overnight.

However, by February the main ski-runs are complete with cold powdery snow over the firm base, providing the best ski-ing conditions for mid-season. As the days lengthen with warm weather, then "spring snow" becomes the standard ski-ing snow surface. This is the delight of Scottish ski-ing, long runs on the firm "corn" crystals that prolong the season to the end of April, and always ski-ing can be found into June and July in the more sheltered corries. In the spring ski-ing season of March, April and May, the longer daylight hours allow more time to be spent on the slopes, with the possibility of undertaking tours over the mountains. Care must always be taken for changes in the weather and the return of sudden deep-winter weather.

DEVELOPMENT OF SKI-ING ON CAIRNGORMS

Ski-ing in the Cairngorms dates back to the early 1900's, when the Scottish Ski Club was founded in 1907 by enthusiasts of the sport, walking and climbing up into the corries, carrying skis, to enjoy a day's ski-ing. During the Second World War the troops of the Snow and Mountain Warfare Training Centre, including Norwegian Units at Glen More, had to do the same thing, only this time for a different reason! In the 1950's ski-ing became more popular, and the walking track from Glen More through the forest and over Windy Ridge into Coire Cas had an increasing pilgrimage of keen skiers and people wanting to try the sport for the first time.

The growth of the Spey Valley as a winter holiday centre made the provision of easier access into the popular ski-ing area a necessity. The road from Glen More was extended up the mountain to the present car park below Coire Cas in 1960. The chairlifts and ski tows have been constructed over the past years as demand has increased for additional facilities to provide adequate ski-ing for the number of skiers now visiting the area. In 1974 a chairlift

91

and ski tow were built in Coire na Ciste from the road extension made by Army Engineers, enabling the originally developed lift system to link with the popular permanent snows of that corrie. Shelter, restaurant and toilet facilities are constantly under review to provide the best service for visitors.

The physical extent of the ski-ing has been changed from the original snowbeds. In order to encourage deeper drifting and widen the runs, snowfences and dykes have been added at strategic points, as well as the actual making of tracks so that the skier can link up the various runs without removing skis. The amount of disturbance to the hillsides has been kept to the minimum in view of conservation and the risk of severe erosion taking place.

The earlier tows were continuous rope-tows that could be placed wherever convenient on the snow. With the building of permanent lifts and tows, there has had to be very careful siting of the uphill lines in order to ensure that the ski-track holds sufficient snow throughout the season. Snowfencing has again helped to build up enough cover.

THE MAIN SKI RUNS

COIRE CAS

The first section of the Cairngorm chairlift gives access to middle station, where the Coire Cas ski tow takes the skier into the head of the corrie underneath the sweep of the Fiacaill to Cairngorm headwall. The popular run here is three-quarters of a mile long, with the long upper section of an easy gradient suitable for learner skiers. The lower part of the run back to the start of the tow is steeper and can become "mogulled" with bumps in the late season. For most of the winter season it is possible to avoid this lower section by turning off to the left down the track cut out of the slope that leads back to the tow and middle station.

FIACAILL RIDGE

To the right-hand side of Coire Cas, the west flanking ridge of the Fiacaill is served by a shorter ski tow just under a half-mile long. From this tow, runs take off to the foot of the tow on both sides of a constant gradient that can be easily handled by intermediate standard skiers. There is no deep watercourse here for very deep accumulations of snow, but the sheltered aspect of the slopes can give excellent ski-ing, particularly when new snow is lying over the old snow base.

THE LOWER NURSERY SLOPES

Areas of snow collect between the middle station and the car park. In deep winter most of the ground here can be covered, but it is

92

possible to link several snow beds and ski back to the car park throughout the season. A small trainer tow and lower tow adjacent to the car park serve the Nursery Slope snows that form here, being especially useful for beginners as the terrain is of a gentle angle and within easy walk of the lift or car park.

THE WHITE LADY

This is the large area of steep snow that forms to the left of the middle station and Shieling Restaurant. The upper section of the main Cairngorm chairlift takes the skier to the top of the White Lady run, and the skier seated on the chair faces out directly on to the run with a grandstand view of the passing skiers down the White Lady. This is one of the steepest runs on Cairngorm, the middle section having the steepest gradient. With heavy ski-ing traffic the run can become mogulled with bumps, but this adds to the challenge of ski-ing the White Lady if you are a competent skier. For many years the White Lady run has provided excellent race courses over the snow, the three-quarter mile run proving a test for National Championships of Slalom and Giant Slalom events. Recently the run has been extended to the side and higher towards the Cairngorm summit by snowfencing, to obtain the International Ski Federation's Race Course Certificate. Electric timing apparatus is permanently installed as part of the high degree of organisation required for the present-day ski racing programme on Cairngorm. On the left hand side of the run a ski tow supplements the chairlift with a linked run from the top into the main part of upper White Lady snows.

A variation of the run down from the top station of the chairlift, is to ski down the start of the White Lady run then turn to the left after 100 yards, following the signs that lead to the Traverse and under the Headwall to join the upper section of the main Coire Cas run. This makes an interesting and less difficult way of ski-ing down from the top for the less proficient skier, and can give a run of well over a mile and a half.

THE UPPER SKI SLOPES

The top of the chairlift also gives access to the large areas of snow that regularly feature the north-east side of Cairngorm and in the upper bowl of Coire na Ciste. These high snows are of a gentle gradient for the most part and serve as a very good nursery class area for ski classes, especially in the spring season when weather conditions are more settled. The Ptarmigan ski tow serves the upper bowl, with a longer ski tow connecting upper reaches of Coire na Ciste with the Ptarmigan area. These snows and those of

93

Ciste Mhearead further round the eastern flank of the Cairngorm summit, hold well into the summer months each year, providing good summer ski-ing for the enthusiastic skier.

COIRE NA CISTE

This steep sided gully leads up to the open bowl slopes that are immediately accessible from the Cairngorm chairlift. A new fixed chairlift, constructed in 1973, now serves the ski-ing in this traditionally popular ski run. This chairlift is in two parts, the first section gives access to the main skiable part of the corrie from the car park, the second section lifts the skier up the side of the West Wall to the start of the open slopes above 3,000 feet. A ski tow then connects this chairlift with the Ptarmigan slopes. The skier has a choice of either taking the ski tow into the upper part of the corrie, or ski-ing down the main bed of the run.

Snow fills in very deep in a normal winter—the steep sides collect any drifting snow as well as protecting it from the worst of the scouring weather—making it one of the longest-lasting ski runs on Cairngorm. The standard is for mainly intermediate to good skiers, with steep ski-ing to be had on the West Wall underneath the chairlift. The length of this run is over a mile long from the Ptarmigan bowl, with an extra three-quarters of a mile length on the lower section back to the car park, when conditions are suitable.

Spring snow ski-ing in Coire na Ciste is one of the special attractions that the Cairngorms offer the skier. The only immediate dangers are that of breaking through the surface into the burn course at the end of the run—easily avoided by keeping to the sides and skirting obvious weak spots. All of these runs are patrolled during the lift operating hours by trained ski patrol staff able to deal with any emergency.

Information is displayed at both car parks regarding the operation of lifts and tows, together with the latest weather forecasts. There are several ski schools that operate on Cairngorm, based from the various centres in Spey Valley. Instruction is of a high standard from the qualified Instructors trained on the courses held each year by the British Association of Ski Instructors.

TOURING AWAY FROM THE LIFT-SERVED RUNS

Several tours can be made starting from the Cairngorm ski area. By taking the chairlift to the top station and then climbing the 400 feet in height to the summit a tour can be made by ski-ing down the south facing slope of the mountain into Coire Raibeirt. By following the edges and tops of Coire an-t-Sneachda and then climbing the flanks and summit of Cairn Lochan, a long snowfield facing west, gives a run to the flat area of the Lurcher's Meadow. Here from this ground overlooking the Lairig Ghru, the shallow corrie of the Lurcher's Burn can give over a mile-long run in most winters. A walk of approximately twenty minutes will bring the skier back to the terminal car park, by the lower ski tow.

A favourite tour in good weather is to visit Britain's second highest mountain, Ben Macdui. A start can be made in the same way by saving climbing time and taking the Cairngorm chairlift and ski-ing over Coire Raibeirt, skirting the Sneachda crags. The upper plateau is usually covered in ample snow for the tour to be made as a cross-country trek by Lochan Buidhe to the summit. There is very little downhill running on this tour, but on a fine day the views all round are magnificent, and a properly equipped party can have a fine day out among the high tops.

Many other tours are possible throughout the other areas of the Cairngorms, but all require additional walking-in time and a good knowledge of where the best snow beds lie.

Even the shortest of tours should be undertaken only by experienced skiers with the correct equipment. Adequate clothing, with spare windproofs, map and compass, and iron rations are the absolute minimum that should be carried before setting off. Notification of the intended route must be left in the special box at each chairlift car park, and due regard paid to the weather forecast. Remember the tops can be suddenly blasted by storms of Arctic severity that can catch out the unwary. Not only does the careless skier endanger his own life by wandering off without careful planning, but he also places in jeopardy the men of Mountain Rescue Teams who willingly go to the assistance of anyone in trouble. In any emergency the chairlift staff should be notified, who will then take the necessary action.

THE SKIER'S CODE OF CONDUCT

1. Never ski alone away from the patrolled run.
2. A skier should never endanger others.
3. Always ski in control. Be able to stop and avoid other skiers.
4. Slower skiers always have the right of way.
5. The overtaking skier must always give a wide margin to the overtaken skier.
6. Avoid stopping in the middle of a run. Whenever possible move over to the side to give a clear passage for other skiers.
7. Do not walk up the middle of runs.
8. Observe all signs placed to control ski-ing downhill and use of lifts.
9. Stop ski-ing when you are tired!

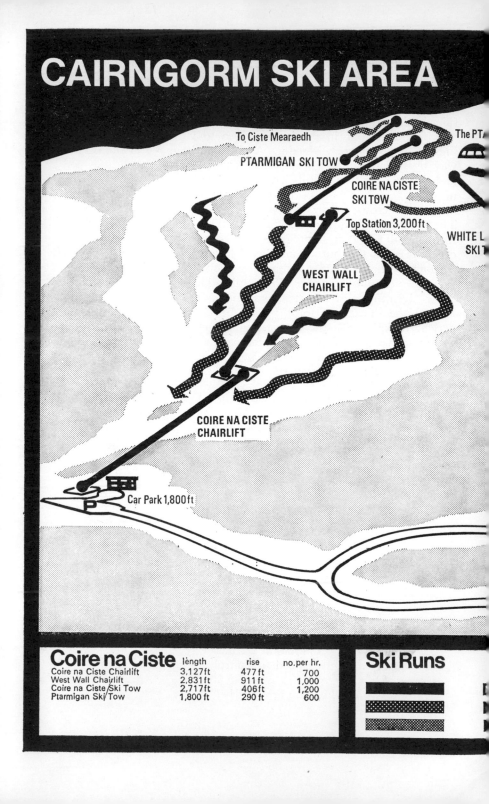

CAIRNGORM SKI AREA

To Ciste Mearaedh

PTARMIGAN SKI TOW

The PT

COIRE NA CISTE
SKI TOW

Top Station 3,200ft

WHITE L
SKI

WEST WALL
CHAIRLIFT

COIRE NA CISTE
CHAIRLIFT

Car Park 1,800ft

Coire na Ciste

	length	rise	no.per hr.
Coire na Ciste Chairlift	3,127ft	477ft	700
West Wall Chairlift	2,831ft	911ft	1,000
Coire na Ciste Ski Tow	2,717ft	406ft	1,200
Ptarmigan Ski Tow	1,800 ft	290ft	600

Ski Runs

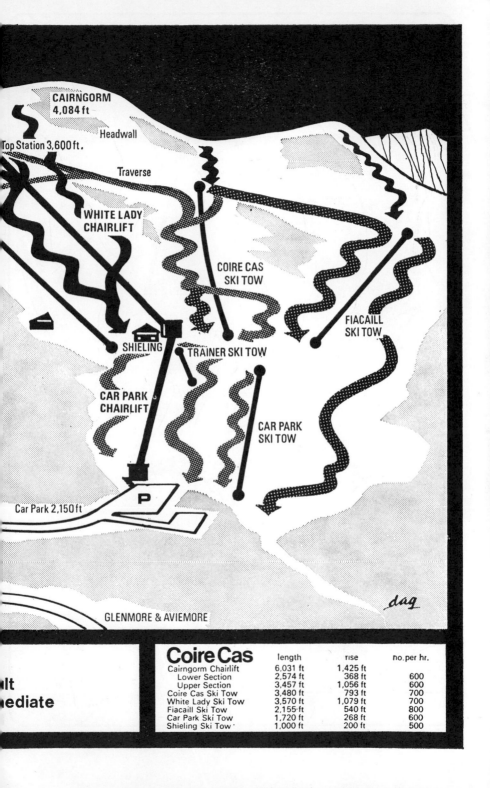

CAIRNGORM
4,084 ft

Headwall

Top Station 3,600 ft.

Traverse

WHITE LADY
CHAIRLIFT

COIRE CAS
SKI TOW

FIACAILL
SKI TOW

SHIELING

TRAINER SKI TOW

CAR PARK
CHAIRLIFT

CAR PARK
SKI TOW

P

Car Park 2,150 ft

GLENMORE & AVIEMORE

dag

lt
ediate

Coire Cas

	length	rise	no. per hr.
Cairngorm Chairlift	6,031 ft	1,425 ft	
Lower Section	2,574 ft	368 ft	600
Upper Section	3,457 ft	1,056 ft	600
Coire Cas Ski Tow	3,480 ft	793 ft	700
White Lady Ski Tow	3,570 ft	1,079 ft	700
Fiacaill Ski Tow	2,155 ft	540 ft	800
Car Park Ski Tow	1,720 ft	268 ft	600
Shieling Ski Tow	1,000 ft	200 ft	500

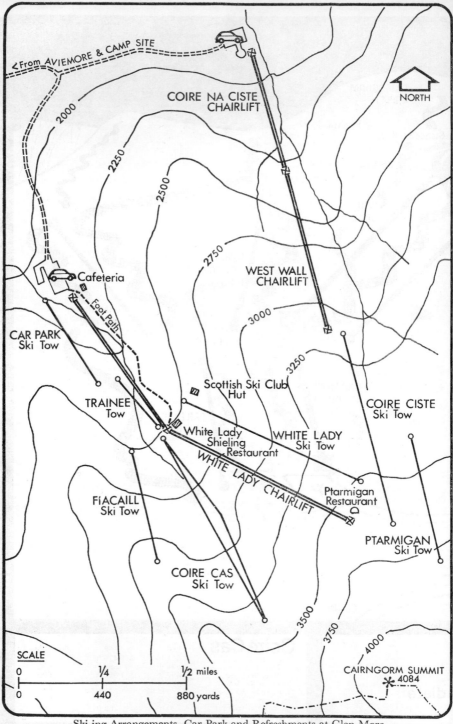

NORTH

< From AVIEMORE & CAMP SITE

COIRE NA CISTE
CHAIRLIFT

2000

2250

2500

2750

WEST WALL
CHAIRLIFT

3000

3250

Cafeteria

Foot Path

CAR PARK
Ski Tow

TRAINEE
Tow

Scottish Ski Club
Hut

COIRE CISTE
Ski Tow

White Lady
Shieling
Restaurant

WHITE LADY
Ski Tow

WHITE LADY CHAIRLIFT

Ptarmigan
Restaurant

FíACAILL
Ski Tow

PTARMIGAN
Ski Tow

COIRE CAS
Ski Tow

3500

3750

4000

SCALE

0   1/4   1/2 miles

0   440   880 yards

CAIRNGORM SUMMIT
4084

Ski-ing Arrangements, Car Park and Refreshments at Glen More

GAELIC PLACE NAMES

Translated by J. M. BANNERMAN

AIRGIOD MEALL	Hill of silver
ALLT BAN	White burn
ALLT NA CISTE	Burn of the box-shaped corrie
ALLT COIRE AN T'SNEACHDA	Snow corrie burn
ALLT CREAG AN LETH-CHOIN	Burn of the lurcher's rocks
ALLT NA DOIRE	Burn of the grove
ALLT DRUIDH	Burn of the shieling (*allt ruidh*)
ALLT NA FEITHE DHUIBH	Black bog burn
ALLT MOR	Big burn
AM BEANAIDH	Burn of corners (*Beannach*) (?)
AN T-AONACH	Expansive heath or moor
ALLT NAN CABER	Burn of trees
AVIEMORE	Great slope (*agaidh mor*)
BADAGUISH	Clump of pine trees
BEN MACDUI (BEINN MAC DUIBH)	Ben of the black pig (*Ben Muich Dhui*)—from its shape
BRAERIACH	Brindled slope (*breach*)
CADHA MOR	Great wedge
CAIRN GORM	Blue cairn
CAIRN LOCHAN	Cairn of the lochan
CAIRN TOUL	Cairn of the barn
CARN EILRIG	Cairn of the deer-walk
CLACH BHARRAIG	Foundation stone
CNAP COIRE NA SPREIDHE	Deer corrie lump (*cnap* pronounced "crap")
COIRE CAS	Steep corrie
COIRE NA CISTE	Box-shaped corrie
COIRE LAOIGH BEG	Little corrie of the calves
COIRE LAOIGH MOR	Big corrie of the calves
COIRE AN LOCHAIN	Corrie of the Lochan
COIRE RAIBEIRT	Robert's corrie
COIRE AN T'SNEACHDA	Corrie of the snows
COYLUMBRIDGE	Bridge of the narrow leap
CRAIG GOWRIE	Rock of the goats
CREAG A' CHALAMAIN	Rock of the pigeons (wild blue rock doves)
CRAIGELLACHIE	Rock of Ellachie

99

CREAG NAN GALL	Rock of the Lowlanders (strangers)
CRAEG GHREUSAICHE	Rock of the cobbler
CRAEG AN LETH-CHOIN	Rock of the lurcher
CREAG LOISGTE	Burnt rock
CREAG MHEADHONACH	Centre rock (pronounced "craig vean")
CREAGAN GORM	Blue rocks
FIACAILL A CHOIRE CHAIS	Teeth of the steep corrie
FEITH BHUIDHE	Yellow bog
GARBH ALLT	Rough burn
GARBH UISGE	Rough water
GLEN MORE	Big glen
INVERDRUIE	Banks of the river Druie
LAIRIG GHRU	Possibly the forbidding or gloomy pass (from *gruamach*)
LAIRIG AN LAOIGH	Pass of the calves
LOCH AVON	Loch of the river (pronounced "A'an")
LOCH A GHARBH CHOIRE	Loch of the rough corrie
LOCH AN EILEIN	Loch of the island
LOCH ETCHACHAN	Loch of the junipers (*aitonnach*)
LOCH MORLICH	The loch of the great sloping hillside (*leacann*) (?)
LOCHAN NA BEINNE	Lochan of the ben
LOCHAN BUIDHE	Yellow lochan
LOCHAN DUBH A CHADHA	Black lochan of the wedge-shaped hill
LOCHAN NAN GEADAS	Lochan of the pike
LOCHAN NAN NATHRACH	Lochan of the adders
AN LOCHAN UAINE	Green lochan
MEALL A' BHUACHAILLE	Hill of the herdsman
MAM SUIM	Rounded knoll
MONADH LIATH	Grey hills
RIVER LUINEAG	Surging river
ROTHIEMURCHUS	*Ràth á mhór ghuithais:* The plain of the great pines
RYVOAN	Bothy shieling (*airidh bhoan*)

100

SLUGGAN	Gullet
SRON AN AONAICH	Point of the expansive moor or heath
STAC AN FHARAIDH	Pinnacle of observation
STAC NA H-IOLAIRE	Rock of the eagles

Note: As guides to pronunciation: The letter *h* softens other consonants which precede it. *ch* and *gh* followed by a vowel are pronounced *h;* otherwise they are guttural. Initial *bh* becomes *v;* so does *mh*. Medial and final *bh, dh* and *th* are scarcely pronounced; they merely lengthen the preceding vowel.

BOOKS ON THE CAIRNGORMS AND STRATHSPEY

Compiled by RICHARD MILNE

ANDERSON, George and Peter
Guide to the Highlands and Islands of Scotland: descriptive of their scenery, statistics, antiquities and natural history. With maps, views, tables of distances, notices of inns, etc. Edinburgh. 1851.

ANDERSON, Peter
Memoranda of an excursion to the Grampians and Strathspey in July, 1863. *Cairngorm Club Journal.* IV, pp. 157–166. 1903.

ALEXANDER, Henry
The Cairngorms: the Scottish Mountaineering Club Guide. Panoramas by H. C. Dugan, J. A. Parker and Gordon Wilson. pp. 218. Scottish Mountaineering Club. 1931.

BAIN, George
The River Findhorn from source to sea. The main object of this work is to draw attention to some of the picturesque features of the River Findhorn. Illus. pp. 254. Nairnshire Telegraph. 1911.

BAIRD, P. D.
Weather and snow on Ben Macdhui. *Cairngorm Club Journal.* 17 (1951). pp. 147–149.

BAYFIELD, Neil G.
Ecological effects of recreation on Cairngorm. In *Nature Conservancy, Range ecology research.* 1971.

BEARE, T. Hudson
Coleoptera at Aviemore at Easter. *Ent. Mo. Mag.* 1907. pp. 272–273.

BEARE, T. Hudson
Coleoptera at Boat of Garten. *Ent. Mo. Mag.* 1869 pp. 267–268.

BLACK, James E.
Coleoptera in Inverness-shire (Newtonmore). *Ent. Record.* Dec. 1906. pp. 321–322.

BORTHWICK, Alastair
Always a little further. pp. 276. Faber & Faber. 1939.

BOYD, William B.
Notes on an excursion to the district of Kingussie with the Scottish Alpine Botanical Club in August, 1877. *Edin. Bot. Soc. Trans.* 1878. XII. pp. 29–34.

BURGESS, J. J. *ed.*
Flora of Moray. pp. 104. Elgin. 1936.

BURTON, John Hill
The Cairngorm Mountains. 1864.

CARPENTER, George H. and EVANS, William
A list of spiders collected in the neighbourhood of Aviemore. *Annals of Scot. Nat. Hist.* III. 227–235, with plate. 1894.

CASH, C. G.
Archaeological notes from Aviemore. *Proc. Ant. Scot.* XLIV. pp. 189–203. 1910.

CASH, C. G.
The Loch An Eilein ospreys. *Cairngorm Club Journal,* 1903–1907. IV. pp. 125–131.

RITCHIE, James B.
The pageant of Morayland. This ︙
in sequence. It is really a coll︙
collected to serve as an introdu︙
story. Elgin Courant. 1838.

ROBERTSON, James
General view of the agriculture in th︙

ST. JOHN, Charles
Wild sports and natural history of ︙

SHAW, Lachlan
History of the province of Moray: ︙
the borders of Lochaber and ︙
Edinburgh. 1775.

SIMPSON, W. Douglas
Portrait of the Highlands. R. Ha︙

SINTON, Thomas
By Loch and River: being memories ︙
Newspaper, Inverness. 1910.

STEVEN, H. M. and CARLISLE, A. ︙
The native pinewoods of Scotland. ︙
1959.

THOMSON, Derrick C. and GRIMBL︙
The future of the Highlands: wha︙
development of productive indu︙
of community, the Gaelic lan︙
Routledge and Kegan Paul. 1︙

TOURIST map of the Cairngorms ︙
1 inch to 1 mile. Ordnance S︙
of interest to tourist.

VALLANCE, H. A.
The history of the Highland Rai︙

WATERSTON, George
Ospreys in Speyside. 2nd ed. E︙

WATSON, Adam
Public pressures in soil, plant an︙
Conservancy. 1967. pp. 38–4︙

WATSON, J. and W.
Morayshire described: being a g︙
1868.

WILSON, Albert and WHELDON, J.︙
Inverness-shire cryptograms ︙
347–356. 1908.

WOOD, Wendy
The secret of the Spey. Illus. p︙
this book lies in the manner i︙
folk-beliefs of Speyside.

CASH, C. G.
Stone circles at Grenish, Aviemore. 2nd Delfour, Strathspey. *Proc. Scc. Ant. Scotland.* XI. pp. 245–254. 1906.

DAICHES, David
Scotch whisky. Andre Deutsch. 1969. £3.15.

DOAK, Andrew
Walks around Carrbridge. Carrbridge. 1911.

DUFF, Patrick
Sketch of the geology of Moray. Map and plates. 72 pp. Oliver & Boyd. 1842.

EDINBURGH UNIVERSITY DEPARTMENT OF GEOGRAPHY
Impact of tourist development in Upper Speyside.

ELLIS, C. Hamilton
Highland engines and their work. Plates. pp. 117. London. 1930.

FINLAY, Ross
Touring Scotland: the unknown highlands (Perth to Inverness). IX. 210 pp. 16 maps. 25 photographs. Fifteen tours to places off the usual tourist track. Fowlis. 1970. £2.50.

FIRSOFF, V. A.
On foot in the Cairngorms. XII. 113 pp. 16 plates. Map. An account of this mountain land, its walks, scrambles, geology, gem stones, climate, botany and wild life. W. & R. Chambers. 1965. 75p.

FIRSOFF, V. A.
On ski in the Cairngorms: explains how the formation of the mountains has given the Cairngorms their very particular character and deals in detail on the changeable climate. Maps and illus. pp. 97. W. & R. Chambers Ltd. 1965.

FORSYTH, William
In the shadow of the Cairngorm: chronicles of the united parishes of Abernethy and Kincardine. Inverness. 1900.

FORSYTH, William
Place names in Abernethy. *Inverness Field Club Transactions.* Vol. IV. pp. 372–379.

GRANT, Angus
Stone circles and other ancient remains in Strathspey. (Duthill). *Inverness Field Club Transactions.* 1877. I. pp. 53–60.

GRANT, E.
Memoirs of a highland lady, 1797–1827. XI. pp. 296. 8 plates. John Murray. 1950. £1.

GRANT, I. F.
Everyday life on an old highland farm, 1769–1782. Shows the life and methods after the earlier agricultural revolution had made itself felt, but before the second revolution in Northern Scotland when sheep farming was immensely extended. Longmans, Green & Co. 1924.

GRAY Affleck
The big grey man of Ben MacDhui. Impulse Books, Aberdeen. 1970. £2. XII. 125 pp. Photographs. The author has gathered together impressive evidence of strange phenomena experienced by climbers on this highest mountain of the Cairngorm range and the one reputed to be haunted.

HALDANE, A. R. B.
The drove roads of Scotland. Maps and illus. pp. 266. Thomas Nelson & Son Ltd. London. 1952.

HALDANE, A. R. B.
 New ways through the g
 nineteenth century.
KNOX, A. E.
 Autumns on the Spey,
 fishers. pp. 171. Joh
LAUDER, Sir Thomas D
 The wolf of Badenoch:
LEES, J. Cameron
 A history of the County
 County histories of S
MACCONNACHIE, Alexan
 Loch an Eilein and i
MACINTOSH, Charles Fra
 Antiquarian notes: his
 parish by parish. M
MACMILLAN, Hugh
 Rothiemurchus. Illus.
A MANUAL OF ANTIQUITI
 Distinguished buildings
 with an outline of the g
 for the information of i
MITCHELL, Joseph
 Reminiscences of my
 David & Charles.
 jector of the Highlan
 London to carry ou
 cerned with roads ar
MURDOCH, J.
 A guide to the Highlan
 men's seats, mounta
 1852.
NETHERSOLE-THOMPSON,
 The snow bunting. C
 maps and diagrams.
 as habits and habita
 two hundred and six
NETHERSOLE-THOMPSON,
 The Cairngorms. A c
PAYNE, Malcolm A.
 The Speyside Project:
 Scotland. 1971.
POUCHER, W. A.
 A camera in the Cair
 Hall. 1947.
REID, William
 Grantown and the adja
 Survey Map. Angus

Pony Trekking

We need a place much more than time
to spend in it, a meeting of the ways
rather than roads down which to strike;
we want to hear of a destination
or of a hill to climb
much more than we want to climb it.

        — Tom Buchan

APPROACHES TO THE PARK
ACCESS ROAD

THE majority of visitors, whether they travel by car, cycle or afoot, approach Glen More by the one road from Aviemore.

 The route from Aviemore leaves the main north road (A.9) about 500 yards south of Aviemore station and is signposted "Cairngorm A.951". Follow this for two miles until one reaches the village of Coylumbridge. Turn half right at this point and follow the main road for three miles, to reach the signposted entrance to the Park. The road continues along the shores of Loch Morlich, beside which there are two car parks suitable as picnic places; one is on the right just after entry to the park, the other, one mile farther on at the eastern end of the loch close to the road and beach with an extension leading into an attractive woodland car park.

A short distance beyond, one reaches the recreation centre of the park, with accesses clearly signposted to the Caravan Park, Loch Morlich Youth Hostel, the Forestry Commission's office and Information Centre with car park, the new Glenmore Lodge (Scottish Sports Council), Norwegian Hostel (Forestry Commission) and Reindeer House.

The main road continues on up to the ski slopes, car parks and chair lifts.

BY ROAD

Aviemore, which is 148 miles from Edinburgh, 145 miles from Glasgow, 83 miles from Perth and 31 miles from Inverness, is centrally placed as regards the main highways through the Central Highlands. First-class roads run northwards to Inverness, Grantown, and north-eastern Scotland; southwards to Pitlochry, Perth, and the Lowlands; and westwards to Fort William. The cyclist will find their gradients easier than the height of the land might suggest.

BY RAIL

Aviemore has a station on the main line from Perth and the South to Inverness and the North, and express trains stop there. The journey from Edinburgh or Glasgow takes 4 or 5 hours; that from London about 10 hours.

At certain times, particularly in the ski-ing season, excursion tickets are issued from Glasgow, Edinburgh, Perth, and other distant towns which allow the holder to spend a holiday in the district at a considerably reduced cost. Details are available from British Railways who issue a brochure entitled: *Ski-ing in Scotland*.

HIRED CARS

The nearest point to the Park at which cars may be hired is Aviemore, distant 7 miles from Glen More Camp Site.

CARS BY RAIL

During the holiday season, British Railways carry cars to the Scottish Highlands, to points convenient for reaching Glen More, by the following services: London-Perth, London-Stirling, Birmingham (Sutton Coldfield)-Stirling, York-Newcastle-Inverness (Summer only).

MOTOR BUSES

LOCAL SERVICES. From April to October buses run from Aviemore to the Chairlift, stopping at Glenmore Caravan Park. The times, as current in 1975, are as follows:—

From Aviemore	..	..	10.00	13.00	15.00 hrs.
From Chairlift	..	..	11.30	14.00	16.30 hrs.

There is no bus service from the end of October to the third week in December. From the fourth week in December until April the times are as follows:—

From Aviemore	..	..	09.30	10.00	13.00 hrs.

Returning from the Chairlift at times depending on weather. Check with Bus Company.

LONG-DISTANCE SERVICES. During the summer months, from mid-June to mid-September only, two services link Aviemore (but not Glenmore) with places to the north and south. One of these is the Glasgow-Perth-Aviemore-Inverness-Elgin service run by Highland Omnibuses Ltd. The other is the Edinburgh-Perth-Aviemore-Inverness service of Scottish Omnibuses Ltd., St. Andrew Square, Edinburgh. Details may be obtained from the respective companies.

AIR SERVICES

The nearest airport is at Dalcross, near Inverness, 32 miles away. There are regular daily flights to Glasgow and London.

ON FOOT

Besides the road routes described above, the Park may be reached by several hill paths, certain of which involve a very long tramp from the starting point; the more important paths are described here.

THE SLUGGAN PASS. This is the shortest route from Boat of Garten. A gravelled track leaves the public road just 4 miles from both Boat of Garten and Coylumbridge and climbs steadily uphill for one mile—giving lovely views over Strath Spey, and then descends gently for two miles to Loch Morlich. Turn left for the Camp Site, one mile on.

FROM NETHYBRIDGE VIA RYVOAN. The road running east, on the south bank of the river Nethy, leads to Forest Lodge, from which point a track, which is a right of way for walkers only, continues southwards to enter the Park through the Ryvoan Pass, and so down to Glen More, the total distance being 10 miles from Nethybridge.

FROM KINCRAIG. A secondary road runs eastward to Feshie-bridge, where some fine cataracts and rock pools may be seen. Beyond the bridge the left-hand road continues northwards past the Forestry Commission property of Inshriach to South Kinrara. Beyond those plantations a well-trodden footpath diverges on the right to climb between two small hills to pine-embowered Loch an Eilein. Bearing left up the loch's western shore, a right-hand turn at the northern end (signposted, "Lairig Ghru" and "Allt Druidh"), followed by a left-fork half a mile further on, brings one on to a track which runs eastwards to the main Lairig Ghru approach path; there turn left and follow that path north to Coylumbridge, whence the right-hand road beyond the bridge runs to Glen More Camp Site. A very pleasant walk of some 15 miles, through forests the whole way; this route avoids most of the tarmac and affords wonderful views of the Speyside hills.

FROM BOAT OF GARTEN one may work eastwards on by-roads through the Forest of Abernethy to Forest Lodge, thence southwards through Ryvoan Pass. This route of about 13 miles is an interesting alternative to the shorter 9-mile approach by the Sluggan Pass road.

FROM BRAEMAR, the easiest of the three possible routes is the Lairig an Laoigh, or Calves Pass, an ancient right of way which runs northwards up the Derry Burn from Derry Lodge in Glen Lui, passes to the east of Loch Avon and Bynack More, and then works round to the Ryvoan Pass and so to Glen More Camp Site. The distance to that point from Braemar is about 26 miles.

The alternative is the famous Lairig Ghru route, a strenuous walk of some 28 miles, involving a climb to 2,733 feet above sea-level at the summit of the pass, and requiring some 12 hours for its completion. After entering Rothiemurchus Forest, the path for Glen More diverges eastward from the Aviemore route, as described in the chapter on hill walks. During the winter months—and indeed well on into late spring—the Lairig Ghru is normally snowbound.

For the seasoned, experienced walker, a fine high level approach is that up Glen Derry to Coire Etchachan, thence north to the Shelter Stone beside Loch Avon. The Feith Buidhe is then crossed and an ascent made to the saddle south-west of the Cairn Gorm summit. From that point there is an easy descent via Coire Cas to the main Cairn Gorm path and so to Glen More Camp Site.

FROM BLAIR ATHOLL, it is possible to reach the Lairig Ghru route at White Bridge across the Dee by way of Glen Tilt, but the total distance of some 36 miles makes an overnight encampment *en route* essential for all but the fittest of walkers.

FROM TOMINTOUL, there is a fine hill track some 22 miles long, via Bridge of Brown, Dorback Lodge, the Eag Mhor gap, Loch a' Chnuic, and the Ryvoan Pass. This is well shown on the one-inch Ordnance maps of the Cairngorms. It involves fording several streams. A longer alternative route ascends the river Avon to link up with the Lairig an Laoigh.

Canoeing on the Allt Mor

Loch Morlich Youth Hostel

GENERAL INFORMATION

CARAVAN AND CAMP SITE

A PUBLIC SITE has been opened at the eastern end of Loch Morlich, occupying a partly open, partly wooded area, close to the sandy beach of the loch. The camp is roaded, with separate numbered stances to maintain a low density of parking. Facilities include water supply, lavatories and a wet weather shelter. Fishing, sailing and canoe hiring facilities on Loch Morlich are available.

The charges, which are on a moderate scale, are shown in the free pamphlet *Forestry Commission Camp Sites and Holiday Accomodation*, which is revised annually.

Payment is made on arrival at the Warden's office close to the park entrance. There is no advance booking.

Enquiries should be addressed to

Head Forester,
Glenmore,
Aviemore,
Highland. (Telephone No. CAIRNGORM 271)

YOUTH CAMP SITE

A site adjacent to the main caravan park is reserved for the exclusive use of youth organisations and for this site advance bookings, at reasonable charges, may be arranged through the Head Forester, Glenmore.

NORWEGIAN HOSTEL

This building was opened in 1970 and is situated on a wooded knoll giving magnificent views to the Cairngorm massif.

It is a well-designed wooden building with a modern kitchen, large common room, drying room and accommodation for 40 people in two dormitories of 20 bunks each, plus two supervisors' rooms with 4 and 2 bunks respectively. Each dormitory unit with its own supervisor's room, showers and toilets is self-contained.

The hostel is equipped with blankets, crockery, cutlery and cooking utensils, but parties must bring their own sheets or sleeping bags. Electricity and hot water is available by pre-payment meter. Firewood is provided free for the common room stove.

The hostel was designed to cater for youth organisations, including schools, colleges and universities.

Accommodation must be booked in advance, with **deposit**.

Charges and other details are available from the

Head Forester,
Glenmore,
Aviemore,
Highland.   (Telephone No. CAIRNGORM 271)

CAMP SHOP

A grocer's shop, operated by an independent shopkeeper, is open all year at the camp site. The goods stocked include bread, milk, tinned provisions, paraffin, postage stamps and a wide range of other goods. There is a tea room adjoining the shop and a sports goods shop on the lower level of the building. In summer a Sub-Post Office is operated in the grocer's shop.

RECREATION ROOM AND CHURCH

A large room, adjoining the Forest Office and Information Centre, is open to visitors as a wet weather shelter and for recreation.

Adjoining this room is a Sanctuary which has been dedicated for religious purposes by the Church of Scotland. Services of an inter-denominational character are held there on Sunday evenings throughout the year and are open to all people interested.

LETTERBOX AND PHONE

There is a letterbox with a once-daily collection outside the Information Centre. A public telephone kiosk is situated near the camp site entrance.

FORESTRY COMMISSION OFFICE AND INFORMATION CENTRE

A prominent sign indicates the Office and Information Centre. The Head Forester or his staff are on duty on week days during the winter and all week in the summer to supply information and answer queries. A wide range of publications is available for sale. The Information Centre has a display illustrating the history and forestry background of Glenmore.

FOREST ROADS, TRAILS AND TREKS

Only two roads within the Forest Park are open to cars and similar vehicles, namely the main public road from Aviemore to the Cairngorm ski-ing grounds, and the branch road leading to the new Glenmore Lodge. The remaining roads within the park are forest roads closed to general wheeled traffic. Except at times of exceptional fire hazard, all the forest roads are open to walkers.

There are three sign-posted forest trails for those seeking leisurely walks within the forest and five more arduous forest park treks for energetic hill walkers. The routes of these are described with detailed directions in pamphlets on sale at the Forest Office.

Where the treks cross the forest deer fences by gate, please close the gate after use.

YOUTH HOSTELS

The old Glenmore Lodge is now a large Youth Hostel named LOCH MORLICH, after the loch beside which it stands, and to avoid confusion with the new Glenmore Lodge of the Scottish Sports Council. It is well-placed at the centre of the Forest Park.

The next nearest hostel is at Aviemore, 7 miles from the Loch Morlich Hostel, but during busy seasons prior booking is desirable there. The large hostel at Kingussie, 17 miles from the Park, is also a convenient centre if cycles, trains or buses are used to lessen the walking distance.

Other hostels are situated at Tomintoul (22 miles), Corgarff (26 miles), Inverey near Braemar (23 miles), and Braemar (28 miles); the distances are those by hill tracks in each case.

Further information will be found in the *Scottish Youth Hostels Association Handbook*, obtainable from the Association at 7 Glebe Crescent, Stirling (price 15p).

HOTELS

A full list of hotels and boarding houses may be obtained from the Spey Valley Tourist Organisation, Aviemore (Telephone No. AVIEMORE 363).

MOUNTAIN RESCUE

There is a First Aid Post and a Mountain Rescue Post at the White Lady Shieling. Anyone in need of help should contact the Inverness-shire Police (AVIEMORE 222), the Chairlift Office, Glenmore Lodge, or the Forestry Commission Office.

There are local Mountain Rescue Teams, based at Aviemore and Glenmore Lodge, and a Royal Air Force Team based at Kinloss. The police co-ordinate rescue attempts.

MISCELLANEOUS

In the Speyside region, within easy distance of Glenmore, there are several commercial outdoor centres providing recreational facilities such as ski-ing, sailing, canoeing, pony trekking, guided tours, adventure courses, etc. Details, brochures, etc. are available at the Tourist Board Office, Aviemore; Forestry Commission Office at Glenmore; or generally advertised in shops and hotels within the region.

A Cairngorm hill race is held annually in the last week of June from the Youth Hostel to the summit of Cairngorm and back. The present record set up in 1972 for the 3,000 feet climb and descent is 72 minutes 47 seconds (a distance of 10 miles). The race, which is held under the rules of the North of Scotland Amateur Athletic Association, is open to all comers. Entries may be sent to the

Secretary,
Cairngorm Race,
c/o Chairlift,
Glenmore,
Aviemore.

114

MAPS

All the Park and the neighbouring areas of the Grampian Mountains, including the Cairngorm National Nature Reserve, are shown on the Ordnance Survey "Tourist Map of the Cairngorms", one inch to the mile scale, price 55p. This is both practical and beautiful with full contour colouring. A recently-published alternative is entitled "High Tops of the Cairngorms" and has metric scales.

Nine-tenths of the Forest Park from Loch Morlich and the Lairig Ghru eastwards is shown on the Ordnance Survey One-Inch Sheet No. 38 entitled "Grantown and Cairngorm". The approaches to the Forest Park from Aviemore and most of the adjacent Rothiemurchus Forest appear on Ordnance Survey One-Inch Sheet No. 37 entitled "Kingussie".

In Messrs. Bartholomew's Half-Inch series, the whole of the Park appears on Sheet No. 51 entitled "The Grampians".

SCOTTISH SPORTS HOLIDAYS

Booklets describing current arrangements can be obtained free of charge from The Scottish Tourist Board, 23 Ravelston Terrace, Edinburgh; The Inverness and Loch Ness Information Office, Church Street, Inverness; or The Spey Valley Tourist Office, Aviemore.

BATHING

The safest and best bathing is at the east end of Loch Morlich where, at the nearest point to the camp site, there is a dry, sandy shore. All bathers, especially non-swimmers, should be very careful as there are deep hollows in the bed of the loch; and no children should bathe unaccompanied by adults. For less hardy enthusiasts, a heated indoor swimming pool is open all the year round at Aviemore.

BOATING AND FISHING

Coarse fishing is available on Loch Morlich and permits may be purchased from the Warden's Office in the caravan park or at the Forestry Commission Information Office. Rowing boats can also be hired for rowing or fishing on Loch Morlich.

CANOEING AND DINGHY SAILING

Cairdsport "Beach Boating Centre" hires out dinghies and canoes from a large boat shed near the loch shore. Visitors with privately owned canoes or dinghies can sail on the loch free, but powered craft are prohibited. A Sailing Club, entitled the Spey Valley Sailing Club, has been inaugurated with a dinghy park and launching facilities at the west end car park. Details of membership can be obtained from the Forestry Commission Information Office or the Spey Valley Tourist Organisation.

PRIVATE RAILWAY

The Strathspey Railway Association are endeavouring to reopen the five-mile section of railway line between Aviemore and Boat of Garten in the Spey Valley and operate steam trains with carriages and buffet car in time for the 1975 tourist season.

THE SKI-ING GROUNDS
CAIRNGORM SPORTS DEVELOPMENT COMPANY

THE SKI ROAD

The A.951 from Aviemore to Loch Morlich continues through the Forest Park climbing steadily up to the ski slopes and is locally known as the Ski Road. It is a fast two-lane highway with a 40 m.p.h. restricted zone at the caravan park and shop section.

As the road leaves the forest out on to the open mountainside, a branch turns left leading to the new Coire-na-Ciste Chairlift Station and large car park. The Ski Road continues to climb uphill to the main car parks and terminal point at a height of 2,000 feet. A wonderful view opens out to the surrounding mountains and westwards over Loch Morlich, the Spey Valley, Aviemore and the distant Monadhliath hills. From the car park it is a short walk to join the complex of chairlifts and ski tows in Coire Cas, described in detail in the chapter on "Ski-ing in the Cairngorms". Charges are levied at this car park. For information the following are relevant details:

Coire Cas		Vertical	
Cairngorm Chairlift	Length	Rise	Capacity
(a) Lower Section	2,574 ft.	368 ft.	
(b) Upper Section	3,457 ft.	1,056 ft.	
	6,031 ft.	1,424 ft.	600 per hour
Coire Cas Ski Tow	3,480 ft.	793 ft.	700 ,,
White Lady Ski Tow	3,570 ft.	1,079 ft.	700 ,,
Fiacaill Ski Tow	2,155 ft.	540 ft.	800 ,,
Car Park Ski Tow	1,720 ft.	268 ft.	600 ,,
Shieling Ski Tow	1,000 ft.	200 ft.	500 ,,
Coire-na-Ciste			
Chairlift—			
Lower Section	3,127 ft.	477 ft.	700 ,,
West Wall Chairlift—			
Upper Reaches	2,831 ft.	911 ft.	1,000 ,,
Ski Tow	2,717 ft.	406 ft.	1,200 ,,
Ptarmigan Ski Tow	1,800 ft.	290 ft.	600 ,,

The chairlifts are automatic two-chair systems where the chairs are stationary at the getting on and off points, which are supervised by chairlift staff.

The ski-tows are the T-bar draglift type. The Shieling and Car Park Ski Tows are suitable for trainees and beginners.

The chairlifts in the two corries form a link system and give lift-served ski-ing well into the spring.

TICKET DETAILS

Single and return tickets are available on any section of the lifts. In the winter season, day tickets are available. Children (17 years and under) and Old Age Pensioners obtain half price. Group party reductions can be made by prior arrangement. Current prices may be obtained from the Information Office in Speyside or from the Chairlift Company

Only adverse weather conditions such as high wind halts the operation of the lifts, otherwise they operate according to the seasonal demand.

RESTAURANTS

The Company operate two restaurants and one snack-bar in the ski-ing area. The snack-bar is situated at the lower Cairngorm Chairlift Station close to the terminal car park.

WHITE LADY SHIELING

This is a large restaurant situated beside the middle station of the Cairngorm Chairlift. The building is heated, providing a licensed self-service restaurant on the upper floor and a large packed-lunch area with hot drinks and snacks on the lower floor. Other facilities are a public telephone, toilets and, most important, a Mountain Rescue Post fully equipped with first aid equipment. The chairlift staff and volunteer helpers are trained to cope with every emergency, from minor mishaps to a major expedition into the wintry hills, to bring in a casualty.

PTARMIGAN RESTAURANT

This is Britain's highest restaurant, standing at 3,656 feet, beside the top terminal station of the Cairngorm Chairlift. On a clear day there are extensive views over the northern mountains. Hot drinks and snacks are served from a self-service counter.

GENERAL

It has taken several years to develop the facilities on Cairngorm, requiring great expenditure and raising of capital, that has been met by public response, government grant aid and share funding.

The Company have paid particular attention to the conservation of the natural flora and fauna and protection of the thin mountain soil by stabilisation works and re-seeding under the guidance of research experts.

Visitors who walk or climb the Cairngorm ski area are requested to follow the sign-posted paths, and avoid areas that are being re-seeded.

GENERAL MOUNTAIN SAFETY

LET THEM KNOW ......

WHERE YOU GO ......

Visitors who set out on long excursions to the higher hills are asked to heed the following notice which they will see displayed beside "posting boxes" at the main starting points of recognised paths.

POLICE NOTICE:

Everyone going climbing or walking in the Cairngorms is specially requested to leave a notice in the box stating:

    Intended route and time of return

    Name and address

    Registration number of car left in park or vicinity.

This information could save your life.

CAIRNGORMS NATIONAL
NATURE RESERVE

By Dick Balharry

CLOSE to the Glenmore Forest Park lies the Cairngorms National Nature Reserve. Between Aviemore in Strath Spey and Braemar in Upper Deeside rises the largest tract of mountainous land over 3,000 feet high in Britain. This is the Cairngorms region, 100 square miles of which form the Cairngorms National Nature Reserve. This reserve has been created to conserve the wildlife of the mountains and wooded lower slopes so that it may continue, helped by scientific management, for the enjoyment of present and future generations.

Is there conflict here? Can the Cairngorms accept an increasing number of visitors bent on a variety of pursuits and still retain the rich resources which are the foundation of their attraction? The Nature Conservancy Council is convinced that with careful planning they can, and Government departments, private organisations and individuals are actively working together to make this possible.

The reserve includes part of the central mass of the Cairngorms. Its high plateau forms a wide, undulating range dominated by broad summits, the highest of which is Ben Macdui (4,300 feet). The edges of the plateau often end abruptly in the vertical cliffs of big cauldron-like corries scoured by glacial action. Steep-sided glens, deepened by glaciers, are entrenched into the plateau, but only the Lairig Ghru cuts right through the mountain block. The imposing scale of the mountains and the striking contrast between the broad summits and the steep valleys and corries give the landscape its unique character.

The south-eastern part of the reserve, Mar Forest, consists of high mountains separated by deep valleys. Here all the streams flow towards the Dee, which has its source at the Wells of Dee close to Einich Cairn (4,061 feet). This area of high plateau is separated from Ben Macdui, three miles to the east, by the huge Garbh Choire of Braeriach and the Lairig Ghru.

The northern part includes the easily accessible and renowned Loch an Eilein. Five miles to the south at the head of Gleann Einich are the precipices of Sgoran Dubh and the huge mass of Braeriach; between them lies Loch Einich at 1,700 feet. The southwest slopes of Braeriach fall to the Moine Mhor, a gently sloping section of the plateau. Westwards again the main mass of the Cairngorms is sharply defined by the valley of the Feshie, which for eight miles forms the boundary of the reserve.

119

Of the 1000 square miles of the reserve, the Nature Conservancy Council owns just under twelve square miles on the estates of Invereshie and Inshriach. The rest, comprising portions of the Rothiemurchus, Glenfeshie, Glen Avon and Mar Lodge Estates, is managed jointly by the Conservancy and the landowners. Without their co-operation and goodwill the reserve could not have been established.

No permission is required to visit the reserve, but restrictions on access may be in force in particular parts of the reserve throughout the year or for parts of the year, for reasons such as the protection of birds during the breeding season, and when essential deer culling operations are in progress during the stalking season. Particulars regarding these access limitations are generally displayed on notices at various places on the reserve. If you are in doubt or require detailed or specialised information, please consult the Nature Conservancy Council Wardens.

Woods of Scots pine cover part of the lower ground of the reserve. The largest ones are on the northern and western slopes of the mountains, but small stands remain also in Mar. Although the original woodland was probably felled in all but the most inaccessible areas at some time or another, the existing trees almost certainly grew from self-sown seedlings and are true natives of the locality. It is probable that these woodlands closely resemble the original Caledonian Forest which once covered most of the lower slopes.

The small remnants of woodland in Glen Derry and Glen Luibeg include some of the tallest pines on the reserve. Although they often set good seed, much of which germinates, the seedlings rarely grow more than a few inches high because of heavy grazing by red deer.

Loch an Eilein, Rothiemurchus, is almost surrounded by pinewoods in which several large trees are at least 250 years old. To the east of the loch there is open moorland with a few scattered pines, and good regeneration occurs in places because this ground is grazed less by deer. Beyond the track to Gleann Einich a broad area of continuous open pinewood reaches the reserve boundary. Woodland also covers the lower slopes of Carn Eilrig, Cadha Mor and Creag Fhiaclach; in places there are quite dense stands, but they thin out towards the upper limits. On Creag Fhiaclach the pines grow at 2,050 feet above sea level, which is probably the highest limit of the native pinewood in Britain.

On the western side of the reserve in Glenfeshie and on the lower slopes of the hills northwards to Creag Follais, there are stands of

Scots pine and much juniper. This is an important wintering ground for deer and natural regeneration of trees is virtually absent.

It is the agreed policy of the Conservancy and the estates to ensure the continuation of the existing woodlands and to restore to woodland at least part of the lower ground which once carried trees.

Except in Glenfeshie, where birch, rowan (mountain ash), alder and willow may be seen, there are few trees other than Scots pine. Juniper occurs locally and in the higher limits of the pinewoods, where it continues upwards to the open moors beyond the level of the trees. The main shrubby plants of the woodland are blaeberry (bilberry), crowberry and heather or (ling).

Scots pine woods are also an important habitat for animals, especially the small and numerous invertebrate species. These occur in every part of living and dead trees and in the shrubs, herbs and needle carpet of the forest floor.

PLANTS OF THE MOORLANDS AND HIGH TOPS

The plants of the Cairngorms are mainly those characteristic of acid igneous rocks, although the less resistant and more fertile schists support a rather richer flora, particularly where the schists are calcareous.

HISTORY OF LAND USE

In addition to serving as a deer forest, Rothiemurchus and Mar were formerly grazed by Highland cattle and sheep during the summer months. The "shieling" system of summer grazing, when people took their livestock to the higher glens, was practised in Gleann Einich and on the flats of Glen Geusachan in Mar. Cattle were also grazed and sheltered in the woods at other seasons. The only cultivation in the reserve was near the Warden's house at Achnagoichan, and by the Allt Druidh and in Glenfeshie, where there are derelict crofts. Timber has been extracted from the woods on Speyside for the past 300 years or more, felling being particularly extensive in the present century because of wartime needs. As elsewhere in the Highlands, moor burning has radically affected the vegetation.

RESERVE MANAGEMENT

National Nature Reserves are maintained under management plans which set out what must be done to conserve the land and its animals and plants. Basic surveys collect information on the climate, physical features and wildlife of the reserve.

In addition there is research into specific conservation problems, which includes experiments to rehabilitate the soil, protect vegetation and animal life, and to improve land management. Much of this research is necessarily long-term, but enough is now known to begin the long process of rehabilitating the Scots pine woods. In parts of the reserve you will see enclosures of deer-proof fencing, inside which young pine trees are beginning to grow up through the heather. These trees may be self-sown, requiring only protection from browsing deer to grow successfully, or they may have been planted as young trees. In Glenfeshie the extensive felling of the native woodland during the 1940s and the subsequent lack of natural regeneration have necessitated a comprehensive afforestation programme. This is being carried out by the estate in consultation with the Conservancy.

The red deer of the reserve are a valuable natural resource, providing sport, venison, skins and antlers; like domestic stock, they require effective management. Much of the grazing ground used by the deer is too high and rough even for the hardiest sheep. Because adult deer no longer have any natural predators in Britain, their numbers, if not kept down by stalking, would rapidly increase until they destroyed their food supply and were forced to invade neighbouring farmland. Man therefore controls them not only for his own benefit but also for the ultimate good of the animals themselves.

RESERVE APPROACHES

FROM BRAEMAR: by the public road to the Linn of Dee, thence, either by the estate road (a pedestrian right of way) to Derry Lodge, or by the estate road (also a pedestrian right of way) running westwards to the White Bridge and thence by the public path northwards up Glen Dee. Cars should be left at the Linn of Dee car park.

FROM AVIEMORE: either by the public road to Loch an Eilein, or via Coylumbridge whence footpaths lead to Gleann Einich and the Lairig Ghru.

FROM FESHIEBRIDGE: either by the public road following the east bank of the Feshie and ending at Achlean, or by the public road on the west bank of the river, ending just north of Tolvah, whence the estate road gives access (on foot only) up the glen.

THE NATURE CONSERVANCY COUNCIL

The Nature Conservancy Council is the government body which promotes a national policy for nature conservation. To this end it selects, establishes and manages a series of National Nature Reserves and gives advice about nature conservation. All this is based on detailed ecological research and survey.

There are now over 130 National Nature Reserves covering more than a quarter of a million acres. They are maintained under comprehensive and detailed management plans.

The headquarters of the Nature Conservancy Council in Great Britain are at 19 Belgrave Square, London SW1X 8PY. Headquarters for Scotland are 12 Hope Terrace, Edinburgh EH9 2AS.

Printed in Scotland for Her Majesty's Stationery Office
by McCorquodale (Scotland) Ltd., Glasgow.
Dd. 132040/3450   K160   8/75